Embedded Analytics
Integrating Analysis with the Business Workflow

Donald Farmer and Jim Horbury

Beijing · Boston · Farnham · Sebastopol · Tokyo

Embedded Analytics

by Donald Farmer and Jim Horbury

Published by O'Reilly Media, Inc., 1005 Gravenstein Highway North, Sebastopol, CA 95472.

O'Reilly books may be purchased for educational, business, or sales promotional use. Online editions are also available for most titles (*http://oreilly.com*). For more information, contact our corporate/institutional sales department: 800-998-9938 or *corporate@oreilly.com*.

Acquisitions Editor: Michelle Smith	**Indexer:** Potomac Indexing, LLC
Development Editor: Jeff Bleiel	**Interior Designer:** David Futato
Production Editor: Gregory Hyman	**Cover Designer:** Karen Montgomery
Copyeditor: Penelope Perkins	**Illustrator:** Kate Dullea
Proofreader: Rachel Head	

May 2023:   First Edition

Revision History for the First Edition

2023-05-15:   First Release

See *http://oreilly.com/catalog/errata.csp?isbn=9781098120931* for release details.

This work is part of a collaboration between O'Reilly and Sisense. See our statement of editorial independence (*https://oreil.ly/editorial-independence*).

978-1-098-12093-1

[LSI]

Table of Contents

Preface

Data and analytics technologies are not only rapidly developing, but they also seem to be constantly in the news. So it is puzzling that industry analysts often say that the adoption of analytics technologies, such as business intelligence (BI), hovers around 25–30% of the addressable market, even while that addressable market has grown. Why is the percentage so low?

Part of the reason seems to be that analytics as a *specialism* may only be relevant to about 30% of the market. But analytics as a way of delivering insight and improved decision making has far greater potential. The new question, then, is how to reach those underserved users.

Our answer, in this book, is that we can embed analytics into the applications that business users work with every day, making analytics part of their regular workflow, not a specialized practice. There will still be a role for analytics experts with bespoke applications, but regular users can benefit from embedding analytic features into other apps.

We think embedded analytics is an exciting field that promises to transform the way we design, build, and use software applications. It is a field that brings together the worlds of data analytics and application design, allowing us to integrate powerful analytical tools directly into familiar applications. The result is a much more intuitive and efficient user experience, which enables users to make better decisions and gain deeper insights into their data. By integrating analytics into the application design process, we can create much more intelligent and effective applications that are better suited to the needs of the user.

This book is designed to provide you with the knowledge you need to embed analytics into your applications and create a more powerful user experience.

Who Should Read This Book

We hope this book will work for a wide range of professionals who are involved in designing, building, or managing software applications that feature embedded analytics. These professionals include:

Application designers
> If you are responsible for designing the user experience of an application, this book will help you understand how to integrate analytics into the application design process. You will learn how to create more intelligent and effective applications that are better suited to the needs of the user.

Analytics professionals
> If you are responsible for developing or managing analytics solutions, this book will help you understand how to integrate your solutions into applications. You will learn how to create more effective analytics solutions that are more closely aligned with the needs of the user.

Developers
> If you are responsible for developing software applications, this book will help you understand how to design and build applications with embedded analytics features. You will learn how to create applications that are more intuitive and efficient for the end user, as well as how to integrate analytics into the application development process.

Architects
> If you are responsible for the overall design and architecture of software applications, this book will help you understand how to integrate analytics into your overall design strategy. You will learn how to create more intelligent and effective applications that are better suited to the needs of the user.

To get the most out of this book, readers should have a basic understanding of data analytics and software application design. Familiarity with programming languages and application development tools could also be helpful, but is not required. Overall, this book is designed to provide practical, actionable insights and advice to help professionals in a variety of roles create more intelligent and effective software applications that feature embedded analytics.

Navigating This Book

Now let's have a look at the structure of the book.

Chapters 1 and 2 explain the background to embedded analytics, describing what a successful project would look like in terms of usability and business impact. We also put a strong emphasis on analytics as a form of *decision support*, so we spend some time describing how to identify the decisions to be made in an operational application and how they can be supported.

Chapters 3 and 4 describe the software and data architectures that are needed to embed analytics effectively.

In Chapter 5 we focus on the types of objects that can be embedded and how these objects can support different business use cases.

Chapters 6 and 7 are concerned with administration and governance. These topics are too often overlooked, so we spend some time explaining the details of what needs to be managed and what constitutes good management and good governance.

Chapters 8 and 9 take a close look at some special use cases. We start with the most ubiquitous analytics tool of all, the spreadsheet. Then we explore machine learning, artificial intelligence, and some emerging use cases related to them.

Chapter 10 is perhaps of greatest interest to software vendors. We look at how embedding analytics in software applications can open up new potential for revenue and even new lines of business.

Conventions Used in This Book

The following typographical conventions are used in this book:

Italic
Indicates new terms, URLs, email addresses, filenames, and file extensions.

`Constant width`
Indicates program listings.

 This element signifies a general note.

O'Reilly Online Learning

 For more than 40 years, O'Reilly Media has provided technology and business training, knowledge, and insight to help companies succeed.

Our unique network of experts and innovators share their knowledge and expertise through books, articles, and our online learning platform. O'Reilly's online learning platform gives you on-demand access to live training courses, in-depth learning paths, interactive coding environments, and a vast collection of text and video from O'Reilly and 200+ other publishers. For more information, visit *https://oreilly.com*.

How to Contact Us

Please address comments and questions concerning this book to the publisher:

> O'Reilly Media, Inc.
> 1005 Gravenstein Highway North
> Sebastopol, CA 95472
> 800-889-8969 (in the United States or Canada)
> 707-829-7019 (international or local)
> 707-829-0104 (fax)
> *support@oreilly.com*
> *https://oreilly.com/about/contact.html*

We have a web page for this book, where we list errata, examples, and any additional information. You can access this page at *https://oreil.ly/embedded-analytics*.

For news and information about our books and courses, visit *https://oreilly.com*.

Find us on LinkedIn: *https://linkedin.com/company/oreilly-media*

Follow us on Twitter: *https://twitter.com/oreillymedia*

Watch us on YouTube: *https://www.youtube.com/oreillymedia*

Acknowledgments

This book has its origins in our work in analytics practices and our conclusion that embedded technologies are critical to the success of this most enjoyable field.

Donald wants to thank those he has worked with closely in teams at Microsoft and Qlik, who were passionate about getting their technologies into the hands of every user. There are too many to list, but special mention must be made of Euan Garden of AppsCo and Microsoft, a tireless advocate, enthusiast, mentor, and friend for many years. Sadly, Euan passed away while this book was still being written, but long conversations with him are reflected in many passages.

Jim would like to thank friends and colleagues at InterWorks for providing the opportunity to work closely with embedded analytics technology and the latitude to write this book.

We must thank the entire team at O'Reilly, especially Jeff Bleiel and Michelle Smith, who steered this book through some perilous waters during COVID, lockdown, and illnesses. Their patience and professionalism, and especially their kindness, have always been a great support and a very focused help.

Finally, it is a pleasure to thank the reviewers of our book: Brian Munz, Majken Sander, and Manca Vitorino. Their guidance was always useful and to the point. They picked up numerous infelicities, large and small. Any that remain are entirely our responsibility.

CHAPTER 1

Introduction to Embedded Analytics

Most of us are familiar today with business intelligence (BI). At one time it was a new and exciting capability, but now—thanks to self-service technologies, the cloud, and the power of in-memory processing—richly featured analytics applications, data visualizations, reports, and dashboards are available to almost any business user who wants them.

However, all of these capabilities typically depend on separate applications. To perform business analysis, you need to open your BI suite. If you want to create a special chart, you use a data visualization application.

Embedded analytics takes a somewhat different approach. The aim of embedding is to integrate visualizations, dashboards, reports, and even predictive analytics or artificial intelligence capabilities inside your everyday business applications. Then, if you are managing a production line, preparing a budget, or reviewing HR issues, you can have analytic insights on hand to guide you.

For a business user, this means that the analytic process takes place in the context of a business process. It also means that the data and the analytic experience become part of your everyday work. This makes analysis more accessible to a business user.

In this chapter, we will review some of the benefits of analytics for enterprises, and we'll also consider what makes for a successful implementation. With that knowledge, we will look at how we could map out a strategy to take us from our current situation to being a more fully informed, analytics-driven enterprise.

Analytics for Business Users and Consumers

There are several advantages to embedded analytics that business users and IT teams appreciate.

From the point of view of an IT team, which is concerned with issues such as security and data governance, embedding your analytics in another application that is already secure has a simple but significant benefit. There is only one environment and one login to be managed; the analytics application does not add an additional layer of complexity. We will look at this topic in more detail in Chapter 6.

Business users will be most familiar with their existing operational applications. Embedding analytics in this well-understood environment affords a nonspecialist user insights and information in a way that works with their existing skills and practices.

In addition to being familiar, it is also more efficient to embed analytics in a commonly used application. If we need to switch from our working application to an analytics application, we interrupt our workflow; we have to open and navigate to another application and may lose focus while we're doing it.

How does this work in practice? In a call center, an operator taking customer calls for support can see on one screen not only the customer record, but also (thanks to the embedded analytics) trends and patterns related to this and similar cases. These patterns (perhaps the customer is calling increasingly often over time) may prompt the operator to route the call to a specialist who can better diagnose and resolve the underlying issues. The result should be a better resolution for the customer and more efficient handling by the call center.

Another example might be a salesperson on the road with an application that helps them select the next customer to visit and optimize the offers they make. They could see, embedded in that application, even on a mobile device, recommendations driven by machine learning.

Other applications may sound more advanced, but in principle are very similar. A doctor may use an embedded algorithm to assist with diagnosis. A production-line manager in a busy factory may need to compare the performance of different machines to see where improvements can be made. An HR person, interviewing an employee with performance issues, may need to compare the employee's work and achievements with those of peers within and across organizational boundaries to suggest a best course of action.

Embedded Analytics for Consumers

We can see some of these principles not only in our work but in our personal use of technology as consumers. Although we grapple with a different set of challenges, as consumers we still make decisions and take actions. As our consumption increasingly moves online, so do our decisions and actions. In ecommerce, you expect to be given recommendations of products that may interest you, the famous example being "customers who bought this also bought that." These recommendations are in fact analytics, embedded inside the web experience of the ecommerce site. We don't think, when browsing for books or clothes online, that it's an analytic experience. Yet analytics are driving our interactions in a way that is so seamlessly embedded, we don't even notice it.

The same is true if we're watching movies online. Our watch list likely includes recommendations made by the artificial intelligence engines of the streaming company. Again, the analytics are there, but seamlessly embedded.

In business we often want to be making decisions that are consciously data-driven. Some users are very interested in their data and like to explore it and make new findings. However, we can learn from a consumer experience when we're dealing with users who must make operational decisions very quickly with the least possible distraction. In that case, an alert or a recommendation can be served up without drawing unnecessary attention to the analytics behind it.

So, one thing we need to think about with embedded analytics is what we're trying to achieve. Are we looking for a simple business outcome? Or are we informing a user with an analytic experience that enriches their use of data, their analytic thinking, and their understanding of the business?

What Success Looks Like

Our discussion so far suggests that what makes for a good embedded analytics experience is variable. In many cases, the best analytic experience will be one that is more or less invisible to the user, like the recommendation engine.

In other cases, we wish to prompt the user into a mode of analytic thinking. Having the analytics or data visualizations right there where they are currently working makes that process more seamless, and, we might hope, will also make it more effective.

So, in each case, there's a slightly different measure of success. For some scenarios we have specific business goals to achieve, but often we just want people to be better informed in their work.

Measurable Business Outcomes

Ultimately, in the business use case of analytics, the business outcome should be straightforward in principle: we make better decisions. Therefore, the most important outcome for embedded business analytics should be smarter, more effective, more impactful business decisions.

Perhaps not surprisingly, measuring a "decision" can be tricky, but in general we should be focusing on a business outcome. For example, we may be looking for increased sales numbers, lower costs, or improved customer satisfaction. Those are the ultimate measures of the success of our process, although it may be difficult to draw a clear line from one decision to the overall outcome.

There are also measures of the process itself: for example, how quickly a decision can be made, how quickly we can process an order, or how many customers or clients our call center can deal with in a day. If we have a recommendation engine, we can measure how often the recommendations are actually accepted, and whether that leads to an increase in sales.

Always, it's important to measure an outcome in terms that makes sense to the business. Simply measuring the process itself doesn't tell us much about its ultimate effectiveness.

Engagement and Adoption

There are important ways in which the process of analyzing can have business advantages in itself, however tricky to measure. Among these merits are the engagement of the user with data and the adoption of analytics software.

Industry analysts often say that business intelligence software only reaches between 25% and 30% of business users. BI software vendors have struggled for over 20 years to increase user adoption. However, the vendors themselves are perhaps part of the problem! It's time to recognize that one of the barriers to adoption is the nature of their specialized tools, requiring a business user to drop out of their business experience and into an analytic experience. This breaks their workflow and disrupts, rather than deepens, their thinking.

Vendors are beginning to realize that one way to increase adoption of and engagement with their software is to embed it in a tool that people already know and use. The advantage of more engagement and adoption should be that your business decision-makers are better informed. We might also hope that business users take an interest in the data, sharing tips and tricks and insights with other users.

Even though engagement and interest may not factor directly into decisions business users make, having greater situational awareness of the business environment, and of the current situation and trends within their department or company, should help.

In fact, sometimes we should be wary of putting precise metrics on these outcomes because there's a common habit of *managing to the metric*, where we focus too much on narrow measures of business value and miss the bigger picture.

Engagement and adoption may also add value through increasing employee satisfaction by giving a broader understanding and adding more business context to what may be a narrowly focused task.

Spreadsheets and Analytics

We have mentioned before that it's important for embedded analytics that the new features live within already familiar software. For many of the people with an interest in analytics—such as financial analysts, marketers, and sales operations staff—their daily work involves a lot of spreadsheets. In fact, for many business people, the spreadsheet is their default analytics tool. Even when they have reports and dashboards, they will often reach for the "export" button so they can load the data into a spreadsheet and do new work.

We don't want to break that paradigm; it's reasonable to recognize that spreadsheets are extremely powerful, flexible, and simple to use. Most people learn to use spreadsheets, including quite advanced features, without any training. So there's definitely a case for embedding analytics into spreadsheets, or extending spreadsheets with analytics.

One way of doing this is simply to provide better visualization features than a spreadsheet can offer natively. Or, we extend the spreadsheet's functions with new capabilities, often integrating with external—and more powerful—analytics engines, especially to handle more data than spreadsheets are designed for.

Another approach is to accept the capabilities, simplicity, and limitations of spreadsheets, but then embed your calculations into another application. For example, you may be able to build a useful mortgage and loan calculator in a spreadsheet (a common scenario for a financial advisor), but with the right tools, you could embed that calculator in a web page or another application, so that your existing or potential clients could use it easily when they browse your site.

It's a little secret of business intelligence vendors, especially of self-service BI apps, that their number one data source is actually not the enterprise data warehouse or cloud applications but the traditional spreadsheet, where the data already exists, and where users can do a lot of the shaping and reviewing of data that's necessary before they build an analysis tool.

Later, we'll talk about several of these scenarios in more detail.

A Game Plan for Embedded Analytics

It may be tempting just to dive into embedded analytics and start inserting charts and visualizations and recommendations throughout your operational systems, hoping to inform your users better. Let's not rush into it! We need a strategy.

We think of this as being more like a game plan than a traditional roadmap. By a game plan, we mean the sort of strategy that a football or basketball team learns before going into a game. They know the strengths and weaknesses of their opponents and their own team. Therefore, they can work out a rough plan of how they're going to approach the problem and how they might respond to developments during the course of the game. But, of course, they never know exactly what's going to happen. They certainly can't predict if the other team is going to have a good or bad day. Maybe this is the day their opponents are at their best, or the day on which they stumble and fall at every opportunity. So any plan must be flexible.

Our goal with a game plan is to give businesses a strategic tool with which they can set a course for a specific technology—in this instance, embedded analytics—while being flexible in how they get there. The first step is knowing where you are starting from.

Understanding Where You Are

The first step of a game plan is to orient yourself, taking stock of your current capabilities, data assets, skill sets, and demands. It's fair to say that when we look at traditional maturity surveys of an entire business, they try to give a single answer that will apply across departments, but that is often too broad a measure to be useful. Different divisions and departments have varying strengths and weaknesses, skills and practices, and indeed, in many enterprises today, tools. They may even have different platforms, especially in businesses that have grown by merger and acquisition.

So step one in designing a game plan is to understand where we are, remembering that organizations can be internally varied and complex, and that each team or department may give different answers.

Setting a Goal

Step two is setting a goal. The same principle, that there is no one-size-fits-all strategy within a company, is true for goal setting too. The manufacturing team or the production team may well have a different level of analytics maturity than the sales and marketing team. So we need to understand not only where every team starts from, but where it needs to end up. What different departments want to achieve with analytics will also differ.

Now you can see why we need that strategic flexibility. Not only is the route from our origin to our destination going to be different between teams, but as we implement tactical solutions for each team, there are likely to be synergies and intersections (and conflicts!) along the way.

So we have unique starting points, varying ending points, and different journeys.

Mapping Out the Journey to Success

The journey that we take from our present situation to our goal can be quite long. It's important, therefore, that we break that journey up into achievable steps.

We strongly suggest that you identify a series of projects, each one taking not more than one business quarter, and define them in such a way that even if you only complete the first one, you will have achieved something. Every step should deliver business value and be in many ways complete in itself. This achieves two very important goals.

The first is that you're constantly adding business value. If for some reason the project has to pause, or even if the project is canceled, you have still achieved concrete goals.

The second is that this continuous process of adding value encourages engagement and adoption with business users because they see the value being added. This approach also increases the commitment and sponsorship of business executives who see progress and a return on investment.

It is much more satisfying to see new features and new capabilities becoming available every quarter than it is to have to wait for a whole year. In the world of embedded analytics, it is straightforward to identify more concrete, less abstract steps that make up this incremental game plan.

However, before we start discussing the architecture and development of embedded solutions, we need to understand a little more about the decision-making process that we are trying to improve. We'll explore this topic in the next chapter.

CHAPTER 2

Analytics and Decision Making

As we consider the role of embedded analytics in business, it's useful to loop back to the question of what we're using analytics for.

One answer is that analytics helps us keep in touch with our business, providing a sort of broad situational awareness for managers and planners. That's a sensible goal, but there is a more practical and direct reason why we need analytic insights: to make better decisions.

To make better business decisions, we need better business information. This has been understood since the first methodical research into decision making at the Carnegie Institute of Technology in the 1950s and 1960s. Even before that, when people first started to create basic financial reports or management reports, the intention to provide better information was implicit. In those days, this process wasn't called *analytics*, it was called *decision support*. In truth, that's still a good name for the practice, because our purpose is indeed to support better decisions.

What Is a Decision?

As is so often the case, a word we use every day can be a little tricky to define. In a business context, we like the definition given by James Taylor and Neil Raden in their 2007 book *Smart Enough Systems* (Prentice Hall):

> A decision...is the act of determining a course of action.

We like this because it so clearly links the act of deciding to the act of doing. Of course, sometimes we may decide not to act, but in business even inaction is a choice with consequences.

Having said that one goal is to support decisions, we need to understand a little more about the decision-making process. There's a wealth of academic research in the field of decision science, often related to probability and game theory, but it's somewhat abstract, so rather outside our scope. For our purposes, we don't need a scientific model, but rather a useful account of an important pattern you can see in most modern enterprises.

Figure 2-1 shows two dimensions of decision making: the number of decisions that we make on the vertical axis and the business value of an individual decision along the horizontal axis. We can see that the curve ranges from a very high number of individually low-value decisions to a small number of individually high-value decisions: that is, from operational to strategic decisions.

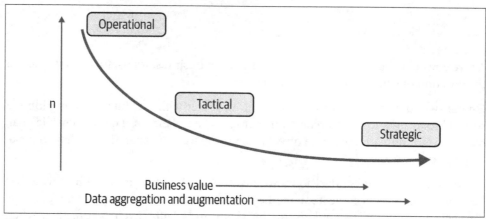

Figure 2-1. Focus on decisions

The decisions vary not only in their value and frequency, but also in the data used to support them and the people who make them. Understanding this variance is important for us when we come to design embedded analytics experiences.

In this chapter, we'll consider the different kinds of decisions that are made in modern businesses, especially where they can be assisted by embedded analytics. We will also discuss a design pattern for analytics, which will be particularly useful when embedding components that need to be impactful but not distracting. Finally, we need to discuss the role of ambiguity in analytics, because it is rare to find our decisions supported by perfect data.

Let's look first at strategic decisions.

Executive and Strategic Decisions

In any business, there are some high-value decisions to be made. What new product will we build? Should we acquire another company? What new markets will we enter?

These high-value strategic decisions each have a significant business impact, but they are not made on a daily basis. These decisions are typically made by executive teams, and the matter may be resolved at an annual or quarterly board meeting or during a monthly management review. Strategy in a well-governed business is not something that changes day-to-day.

The data that supports such decisions is highly aggregated. The quarterly board meeting does not get hung up on the details of every sales transaction, but rather considers global or departmental sales over the preceding period, summed up, averaged, and trended.

Not only is data for strategic decisions aggregated in this way, it is also augmented with a lot of external information. Executive decisions are rarely made by looking at only one data source or one narrow domain of business. Strategy is informed by all sorts of data, which may not even be captured in a structured format. For example, a strategic decision may be influenced by competitive intelligence about rival businesses, the state of the economy, questions of political stability, and the hopes of the business leaders. We will look at executive decisions in more detail in Chapter 8 when we consider how spreadsheets, the executive tool of choice, can be embedded.

Operational Decisions

If we look now at the other end of the spectrum, at operational decisions, we can see that there are very many of them. Indeed, there will be thousands of operational decisions made every day in a large business.

An operational decision is a choice made in the course of business that is very limited in scope and individually has a low business value compared to a strategic decision. Which customer do you visit next? What products do you present to them? What discount may you offer? What action do you take when this alarm goes off? Do you approve a loan for this customer?

Of course, in an important sense, operational decisions *are* your business in action. This is how your business operates.

Operational decisions are typically made with a relatively limited amount of data from well-defined data sources. There may be no external information used at all. In all these ways, they are almost exactly the opposite of a strategic decision. The decision-maker, rather than an executive, may be a salesperson, machine operator, call-center representative, or clerk.

Operational decisions are a prime use case for embedded analytics. If you need to respond to an alarm or to make an offer to a customer on the phone right now, it's extremely useful to have some context or a recommendation that helps you make a better decision. Otherwise, you'll likely just respond instinctively to a relatively low-information event.

For these reasons, throughout this book, we will often focus on operational decisions and how we can improve and enhance them with embedded analytics.

Tactical Management Decisions

As Figure 2-1 shows, in the range between operational and strategic work, we have tactical decisions. These decisions are typically made by those we sometimes call (not always as a compliment) middle managers. Despite their reputation as bureaucrats, the middle manager role is extremely important in business decision making. Middle managers work within a scope that aggregates operational decisions to a point where patterns, trends, and exceptions can be found. From there, the tactical decision-maker sets the direction of the business over a workable period of time, which may be days, weeks, or months, rather than the yearslong outlook of strategic planning.

For example, a sales manager, unlike the VP of sales, will need access to all individual sales transactions, perhaps digging in to detail if even one item looks notably wrong or exceptional. In this way, tactical decisions are made with aggregated operational data and perhaps with some augmentation from sources such as HR data. Nevertheless, the scope of tactical thinking is much tighter than that of strategic decision making.

Middle management decisions are the key focus of traditional business intelligence. It is for this kind of work that most reporting and dashboard tools have optimized their user experience over the last 20 years. In fact, this middle management focus is also the reason business intelligence has been limited in its adoption, because there are a limited number of tactical decision-makers.

The Limits of Business Intelligence

In 2017, the Gartner analysts Cindi Howson and Rita Sallam said (*https://oreil.ly/ HEB9h*), "Pervasive business intelligence remains elusive, with BI and analytics adoption at about 30% of all employees. Data and analytics leaders wanting to extend the reach and impact of BI and analytics in their organizations should deploy modern BI platforms, leveraging mobile and embedding capabilities."

There is a reasonable case to be made for extending the reach of BI, but we're convinced that we'll do that by focusing on improving decision making, not just by increasing adoption in itself.

In contrast, there are a very large number of operational decision-makers, and those are the people we are trying to reach with embedded analytics. That's not to say there's no role for embedded analytics in the world of the tactical manager or strategic executive: we'll look at some of those scenarios when we consider reporting and dashboard solutions.

For now, how can we start to support decision-makers with data and insights? In the next section, we'll share some patterns that will help.

A Design Pattern for the Analytic Experience

In 2007, Marcia Bates, a leading researcher at UCLA's Department of Information Studies, analyzed the components of browsing behavior, specifically in a library. Her paper, "What Is Browsing—Really?" (*https://oreil.ly/JUqjr*), is fascinating. Bates explores the research in some detail, but we have found a simplified model to be useful in our own work.

Please note that as we describe this model, all the good points really come from Bates's work—it's a paper worth reading. Any inadequacies are the result of over-simplification.

Whether we are considering analytics just for information or, as in our case, as an input to decision making, the pattern shown in Figure 2-2 works well.

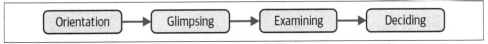

Figure 2-2. A simplified model of the analytic experience

Orientation

The first step in browsing—and in analysis—is to know where you are, to orient yourself in the information environment. In a library, that would involve knowing which subject section you are in and how to find your way to other sections.

When working with analytics objects embedded in an application, there are similar questions. What are we looking at? Let's say it's an analysis of product sales. What products are included? What geographies? What years are shown? We should not overwhelm the user with "helpful" indicators because they are more likely to be lost in the detail than helped. (Think of how difficult it can be to make sense of a road junction with too many lights, signs, and markings.) Two or three key pieces of information should help a user determine what they are looking at.

Orientation should also afford a user some sense of how they can move through the information space. For example, if you're looking at today's call volume, how could you find out the numbers for yesterday or the week before? Is that information available?

It is beyond our scope here to describe all the ways in which the user experience can provide these capabilities. In fact, we don't need to, because when we embed analytics in a host environment or application it is most useful if the orientation and navigation features of the analytic components more or less follow those of the host application. In this way, the experience is more familiar and simple to learn while reducing the cognitive burden for the user of switching between environments.

Glimpsing

The original example of a library (or a bookstore, if you prefer) serves us well here. If we are looking for a book on how to run good meetings, we can surely orient ourselves toward the business books section. But how will we find that meetings book? There will likely be hundreds of volumes on all sorts of topics, perhaps organized by author.

If we have time, patience, and some knowledge of the system, we may consult a catalog. Otherwise, we're much more likely to *browse* (thus the title of the paper), not looking carefully at every book in turn, but rather letting our vision drift over the shelves until something catches our eye. We *glimpse*, perhaps, the word "meeting" in a book's title. And, just as we glimpse the title, we will also take in the author's name, design features of the cover, and so on.

In analytics, glimpsing is an essential step in making sense of data, especially when we are looking for insight or new information. In the scatter plot shown in Figure 2-3, it's easy to see that some values, called *outliers*, are standing apart from the majority of data points. They enable us to glimpse what may be interesting or important.

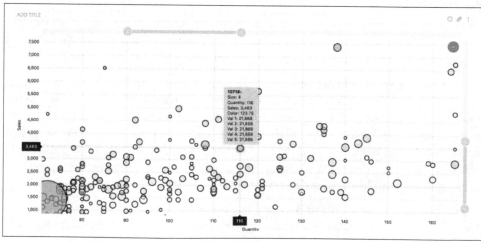

Figure 2-3. A scatter plot where outliers can be easily glimpsed

Similarly, in the time series visualization in Figure 2-4, we can glimpse several useful characteristics. The overall trend shows sales increasing over time, but there is one short period where sales show a significant drop before recovering: why might that be? And we can glimpse a recent spike in values; perhaps that's a useful data point to explore.

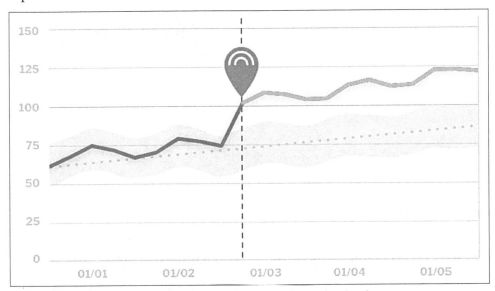

Figure 2-4. A time series chart enabling spikes and dips to be clearly seen

As you can see, certain visualizations are particularly useful for enabling these quick insights. In fact, choosing the right visualization for your data should involve a consideration of how the information will be glimpsed and then, having seen something potentially interesting, how it will be examined. This is the next step in the model.

Examining

Back in the library, having glimpsed a book about meeting culture, it is time to see if it will be a useful choice. So we take the book from the shelf and examine it. Note that we don't read the whole book while we're there in the library. We may look at the table of contents, flip through the chapters, read the short marketing blurb and enthusiastic quotes on the back cover. Has it got diagrams? Exercises? An index? Examining helps us to understand if this book is indeed as useful as we hoped.

In our visualizations, we can do something conceptually similar. Having glimpsed a data point or a trend we think is important, it is time to examine it.

Some tools make this easier than others. In Figure 2-5, by hovering the mouse over the data point in question, you can bring up a small panel with more information.

That's certainly useful and better than overloading the visualization with all that extra detail presented up front.

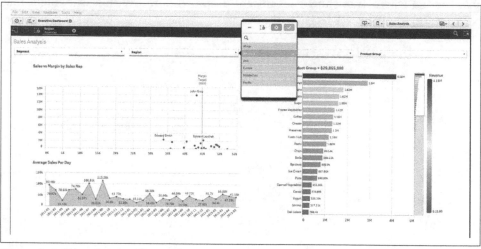

Figure 2-5. Examining a data value

The Navigational Scope of Embedded Analytics

In these examples, when we examine some feature of the data that we glimpsed, we are given more information about it. Some business intelligence tools enable you to do much more. For example, having examined sales at the level of the region, you might expand your view, look at sales for the entire enterprise, and then trace a new path into a different region. Strategic and tactical decision-makers do this frequently because they are examining data at a higher level and need to make comparisons across a much wider span of the business.

However, if you are a salesperson trying to select which customer to visit next, and you are using an embedded visualization to help with that decision, you are unlikely to gain much insight by comparing your own work to overall sales at a global level or in another region. You will do best to focus on scenarios that remain admittedly small-scale but relevant to your own decisions.

When embedding analytics, we must bear in mind that we're not embedding a complete BI environment that can address any issue in the enterprise. We are supporting a specific class of user as they make specific decisions.

To enable this tighter focus—and to prevent distracting users—embedded analytics are typically much more restricted in scope than traditional, general-purpose BI tools.

Another example is presented in Figure 2-6. In this case, rather than just hovering over a part of the visualization for more information, you can click on the data point in question and the whole view changes. You have gone from looking at sales by region to examining sales by one particular salesperson in that region. We call this kind of interaction *drillthrough*. It's a critical capability of any business intelligence tool.

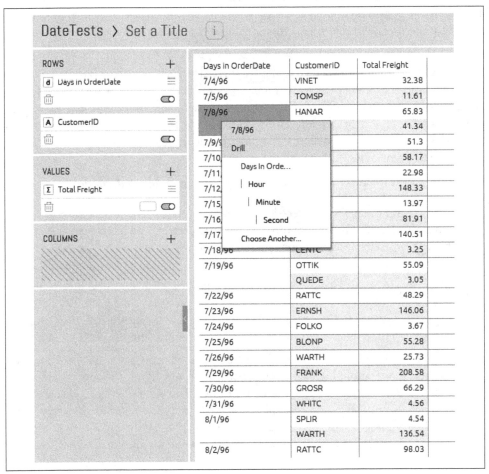

Figure 2-6. Drillthrough in action

Deciding

When Marcia Bates investigated browsing in the library, the last step she identified was called *acquiring*. The person browsing literally acquired an object to use, checking out a library book to read it.

In our case, we are not going to take our data to the front desk to be stamped and later returned. But, having glimpsed something interesting and having examined the data, we now have an insight, and it is time to do something with it. It's time to take an action, to make a decision.

As we've emphasized that we are supporting decisions in our work, you can imagine this step is absolutely critical to the success of embedded analytics. In fact, this subject is so important that a large part of Chapter 3 will discuss how we model the components of a decision and then enable the decision to be made with analytic insight.

For now, it is fair to point out that this final step has not been handled well in analytics tools. For a long time our focus was on the challenges of our day—getting good-quality data into the hands of the business users and enabling them to explore it and visualize it. We did a good enough job, but the technology and the user needs have moved on. Today, we need to integrate this decision-making step more directly into the user's workflow.

There are four ways in which users can move from *examining* to *deciding*:

- Users can simply make the decision themselves—in their heads, if you like—and then go to another tool or another operational environment to take the action. This is how users made decisions with traditional BI tools.

- It is common for dashboards and some reports to enable users to share a visualization in email, or through a chat application, or even by clipping or sharing the analytics object into a presentation slide. Sometimes this capability is tightly integrated, but often it is only a loose capability. It still requires the user to make an observation in the analytics tool and take action elsewhere.

- Some BI tools enable extensions to the analytic environment that can integrate links to an operational application. This is often through a process called *write-back*. We will discuss write-back in more detail in Chapter 4. In a sense, this approach is the very opposite of embedded analytics: it embeds operational capabilities into the analytics toolset rather than analytic capabilities into the operational environment. There are good scenarios for this that we will discuss later.

- Finally—and our main focus here—if the analytics object, such as a visualization, is embedded in an operational application, the user can take the action right there on the same screen, without switching environments or losing focus. As a salesperson, you might see some outliers in your customer analytics, perhaps clients you have not called in a long time. Right there, in your customer management application, you can decide to initiate a phone call, make notes, and deal with those customers directly.

This model of browsing is powerful and practical, in part because the experience is very natural for us. We use it in a library. In fact, with a little thought you will recognize the pattern in many of our activities, such as choosing a movie to stream or grocery shopping. However, we do want to emphasize that the pattern is simplified from real-world experience to make it a little easier to apply in our design work.

One important aspect of data and decision making that this browsing pattern glosses over is the common problem that our data does not always lead clearly or cleanly to a single, simple decision. Data, in the real world, is ambiguous.

Ambiguity and Analytics

Human beings are not comfortable with ambiguity. Research into our neurological reactions to ambiguity shows our amygdala, which controls our flight or fight instinct, lighting up as we become emotionally and physically uncomfortable with uncertainty.

In addition to this discomfort, ambiguity is simply not persuasive. As J. M. Coetzee wrote in *Diary of a Bad Year* (Penguin), "If you do not already think in probabilistic terms, predictions emerging out of the probabilistic world seem vacuous." General MacArthur did not leave Manila saying, "I will probably return."

Business intelligence has mostly sought to remove ambiguity and uncertainty by favoring clarity over complexity. The best-known example is the claim of data warehouse architects to deliver *a single version of the truth*. This implies, in its very phrasing, the existence of alternatives to be suppressed. Certainty is rewarded.

Even where uncertainty is unavoidable, we often prefer the artificial clarity of a fixed value. It's common to see dashboards that predict budgets and expenses down to the very cent, as in Figure 2-7.

Of course, we don't believe that we will ever behold sales of exactly $7,493,087.68, but we lack the tools and, for many people without a background in probability, we lack the vocabulary to bring more realistic, more *ambiguous*, outcomes into focus.

At best, everyone involved understands this as a game of self-deception. Nevertheless, behind the comfortable illusion lurks the danger of the fallacy of false precision. We may place undue trust in these forecasts because they look accurate, forgetting our own part in the trick.

Today, we are only fooling ourselves. But as machine learning and artificial intelligence are innately probabilistic, our businesses are rapidly reaching the point where such illiteracy will severely limit our work and success. We don't all need to become data scientists, but we do need to get better at communicating uncertainty in our work.

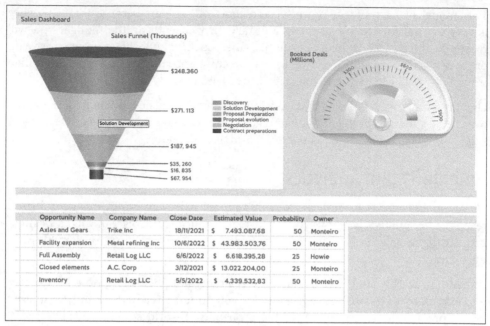

Figure 2-7. A dashboard of unrealistic precision

Figure 2-8 shows an example of a visualization that represents ambiguous data in a helpful, easily understood way.

Although we cannot precisely know what the continental populations will be in the future, we can make reasonable predictions, as shown in this visualization. It also shows, in a simple way, the range of potential variance around that prediction—the ambiguity. Yet this is not a technical chart, with complex formulas and detailed visualizations of error. Almost any reasonably data-literate user can understand it. And more importantly, it can lead to better decisions. For one thing, we can see and interpret very easily the potential range of scenarios.

Ambiguity is a complex issue. A full treatment of the implications for business decisions is somewhat out of scope for us. However, understanding that the problem exists and that there are ways to address it will be useful when we come to design embedded analytics experiences.

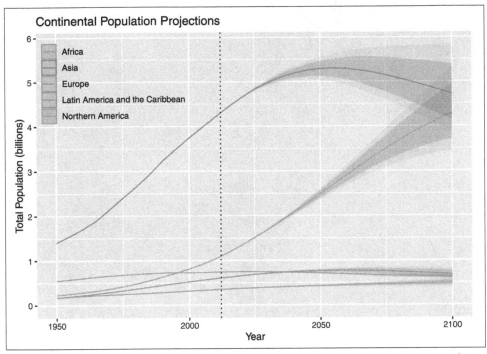

Figure 2-8. A simple, but compelling, visualization of uncertain data, by Adrian Raftery of the University of Washington

Summary

In this chapter we have reviewed the different kinds of decisions made in the modern enterprise. We have seen that strategic decisions are made with a wide variety of inputs and so rarely benefit from embedded applications—but look out for spreadsheets, which are still an important tool for executives.

Tactical and operational decisions (the decisions of line managers and their staff) are those which benefit most from embedded analytics. The pattern of Orientation–Glimpsing–Examining–Deciding greatly helps in making analytics accessible and effective.

Finally, we considered how we can deal with ambiguous and uncertain data, which is increasingly important as we make more use of predictions and other machine learning features in our work.

Now it is time to get started planning our embedded analytics.

CHAPTER 3

Architectures for Embedded Analytics

Having looked at the nature of decisions and a design pattern for analytics, how do we start to put together an embedded analytics solution? In this chapter we will give an overview of some architectural features to consider. We will also look at some benefits and weaknesses of common approaches.

Elements of Embedded Analytics

When thinking about how to approach embedding analytics in your applications, look for several common elements, as described in this section.

Data Connectivity

We will consider the topic of data for embedded analytics in much more detail in Chapter 4. But for now, we should recognize and understand that simply being able to connect your data source is a critical capability of any analytics solution. This is not always as obvious as it may sound.

When we embed analytics into operational systems, we often connect to legacy applications that the business has been running for years. Or perhaps we need to access data in custom applications. And in both these cases we may have to integrate both operational and analytic data. If you cannot connect, in all of these scenarios, you will fall at the first hurdle.

The Analytics Engine

Analytics is more advanced than reporting because the pattern of Orientation–Glimpsing–Examining–Deciding is predicated on interactivity, especially in the examining phase. Often, when we have glimpsed a potential insight and examined it, we discover things are not quite as we thought. So we return to glimpse another, related insight to examine again. This process can prove quite convoluted. Think of the steps you go through searching for a restaurant or hotel online: internet search engines employ our analytic pattern too!

An embedded report has limited scope for this kind of interaction. You may filter or sort the data in the report, in the same way as a regular report might be filtered or sorted. There is nothing especially "analytical" or insightful about an embedded report. The report server may need to scale substantially, but it rarely has complex calculations to perform: any advanced or involved aggregations or predictions will generally be calculated outside the report server by the analytics engine. Similarly, a visual component added in code may be used only to display results, and not have any real analytics behind it.

Embedded analytics, on the other hand, may include quite sophisticated options for selections, navigation, and even custom queries or calculations. The visualizations may display data in complex and demanding ways, perhaps enabling us to zoom in from a summary to fine detail. In such cases, the analytics engine is critical.

What is the *analytics engine*? Generally speaking, it's a system for performing queries against one or more data sources that includes specific functions for analyzing data. An online analytic processing (OLAP) system can typically perform numerous aggregations, such as computing sums, averages, and minimum and maximum values, across large volumes of data with near-instantaneous performance. And, of course, the aggregations may be much more complex than these examples. Other analytics engines may have particular knowledge about time series data and be able to perform calculations such as year to date and same period last year with a simple query for developers and great performance for users. More recently, we've begun to see analytics engines with features for machine learning algorithms and data science.

Expect an analytics engine with high performance, preferably one with query optimization, to take best advantage of available resources and the best methods of computing results.

Branding the User Experience

It is a common requirement that an embedded solution should not look like an embedded solution! Designers generally want the analytics to look completely consistent with the host application. This expectation may require that navigating, selecting, editing, confirming changes, and so on should all behave the same way in the embedded environment as in the host.

Moreover, the host environment may be branded with logos, corporate standard colors, and preferred typefaces. When we *white label* the user experience, all these elements will look the same in the embedded analytics objects. This is a common requirement, although we are skeptical of its value: it can be a useful nudge to a user's curiosity to recognize that this chart or that table is a special object worthy of attention. It's similar to pulling out a quotation in writing, not only to show that this is another author's words, but also to give them some authority as being noteworthy. On the other hand, we understand the resistance to the other extreme, where the analytics vendor's name, logos, and UX preferences are all visible in what should be an unintrusive embedded component.

Seamlessness Is Not What It Seems

A term you will come across often when researching user experiences or any architectural integration is *seamless*.

Seamlessness, we are told, is a virtue: the idea being that when we switch from one context to another in our work, the cognitive effort required reduces our productivity and distracts us. The solution is an environment where we do not need to switch context but see all our different scenarios working together as a unified whole, like in a seamless garment.

Metaphors can be tricky. Seams are, in fact, important. They don't merely hold together a garment stitched from pieces of material. Seams give shape to our clothing, so it drapes properly and moves with us. Seams give strength. Seams are practical.

So, too, in software design. Sometimes a user will not want to switch context; they just need a quick reminder of a number or to glimpse a trend. But at other times, we absolutely do want the user to switch context: they should be aware that *now I am doing analytics* and this involves a slightly different practice from my regular work.

Think carefully, therefore, about seamless experiences. What does the user need to know about what they are doing? Will a clear transition from one mode of thinking to another help them? Sometimes, you need a seam.

Developer Resources

In this chapter we will review several different criteria that may influence your choice of embedded analytics architecture. However, in many cases we have seen the decision come down to just two simplified, if rather extreme, parameters. First, can I connect to my data? That is essential, of course. But also, can my developers do this work effectively? Have they the skills, the resources, and the time?

In general, we may prefer an embedded architecture that reuses as much of our existing effort as possible, whether in data, analytics, security, or application management. Or, we may be required by legislation or best-practice guidelines (for public departments and certain highly regulated industries) to ensure that security and access control run based on a particular system, or that certain user experience and accessibility requirements are adhered to.

Scalability

When embedding analytics in operational applications you should be aware of two different forms of scalability.

First—and most familiar—is the volume of data that the analytic system can handle. When vendors talk about large-scale solutions this is generally what they mean. At the high end, modern engines are designed to handle even petabytes of data, but because the design of analytics engines varies widely, it is useful to ask if your candidate system can handle all the data it needs to. This is unlikely to be a problem if you are integrated with, say, an HR system or a customer record system: you will almost certainly not have enough employees or customers to cause any issues with even a basic reporting system. However, if you're connecting to an enterprise data lake and summarizing big data, such as web logs or ecommerce transactions, then scale really can prove problematic, especially for in-memory analytics engines that must hold all the data at once to work with it effectively.

A second form of scalability is the number of users who may connect to the system, especially simultaneously. This often varies throughout the day and the week, as discussed in the following sidebar, but there may also be seasonal trends depending on your business.

The 9 a.m. Problem

Donald Farmer

I began working with commercial enterprise servers in the 1990s. Previously my work had focused on complex, but smaller, scenarios, often in research. But when designing reporting and analytics applications for large clients such as oil companies, retailers, and health care providers, I became familiar with a problem of scale. At 9 a.m. each weekday, and especially on Mondays, almost every manager would log in to the system and refresh their critical reports. This was the peak load on the system, and we quickly learned that simply throwing resources at the problem—such as larger servers—was not a popular solution, mainly because it was so expensive. We used a variety of techniques, including predictive preprocessing, caching, cache sharing, and just-in-time processing, to make it work.

You may not have this problem today. In fact, in these days of cloud computing you should not. Your cloud service provider should be able to provision truly elastic scalability that is efficient and cost-effective. However, you should take care to model this scenario—calculating what peak demand will look like—and ensure that it is indeed reliably implemented by your cloud provider and analytics engine.

Security

In Chapter 6 we will dig deeper into the security implications of embedded analytics, and in Chapter 7 we will also look at some topics relating to data governance. Here, it is important to point out some key criteria to consider when choosing a platform:

- Ensure the analytic system can implement the right protocols for your needs. Look for standard integrations such as Lightweight Direct Access Protocol (LDAP), OAuth, or Active Directory.

- Role-based security is critical. You must be able to configure permissions to see and work with data based on the role of the user. Even better, users should inherit these permissions directly from the hosting application, so you don't have to reinvent the wheel and define the same security requirements twice.

- Single sign-on (SSO) could be essential for you. Requiring users to sign in to their host application and then sign in again to their embedded analytics platform is a clumsy and error-prone process. SSO enables just one login for access to all the related applications. This is not merely a user experience issue. Any workaround that involves managing different user accounts (the host app and the embedded app) without SSO could result in a developer taking shortcuts, hardcoding usernames and passwords, or even reducing security precautions in the embedded app.

- Will the analytics need to be accessible externally in a customer web application? If so, the environment should support embedding in web applications, provide the necessary security measures, and have the scalability and performance to handle a high volume of external users.

- Logging is also an important consideration, as it helps with troubleshooting, monitoring performance, and identifying usage patterns that may cause security issues.

Administration Tools

When you must manage all these elements—data access, security, scalability, and the user experience—you will appreciate effective administration tools.

One important administrative feature is the scheduling of updates and data refreshes. Particularly when working with a host application that also refreshes on a schedule, be sure that you can synchronize, share, or reuse schedules as needed.

IT are people too! In all our talk of the user experience and the need for effective business user tools, it is easy to overlook the needs of IT. But let's remember that IT teams work day in, day out administering servers and applications. They will also suffer from context switching if user experiences are badly designed. Moreover, if they are fatigued, stressed, or just working with clumsy and inefficient tools, their mistakes can have consequences that extend far into the enterprise and might even cause user adoption of the solution to fail altogether. So please, consider your IT staff: they deserve—and they need—excellent applications too.

Embedded Analytics Platforms

Having described some of the elements of an embedded platform, we can now look at different approaches to embedding, each with its own benefits and weaknesses. We will consider component libraries for developers, enterprise reporting and BI platforms that can also be used for embedding, and finally, purpose-built platforms specifically geared for embedding.

Component Libraries

It can be very tempting for developers to "roll their own" solution, building the entire embedded analytics infrastructure from scratch. The temptation arises because component libraries for visualization are very attractive, offering a wide range of chart and graph types from the most basic to the most sophisticated.

Perhaps your needs are simple: your budget is restricted, your configuration is static, and you don't expect to integrate more demanding analytics in the future. In such cases, you can certainly look at component libraries as an effective way to get started.

Equally, if you have a specific need for a specialized and sophisticated chart type, then a visual component library such as D3.js (*https://oreil.ly/5RKot*) or Highcharts (*https://oreil.ly/WTA6V*) (see Figure 3-1) may be your best, or indeed only, option.

However, there are significant drawbacks to visualization component libraries as a practical solution for businesses focused on operational and tactical decision making. Development can prove time-consuming because every component must be customized in code, with security and administration also defined in code at a component level. While this may work as a quick way to get started, maintenance becomes a real problem when, for example, data connections must be redirected to a new source.

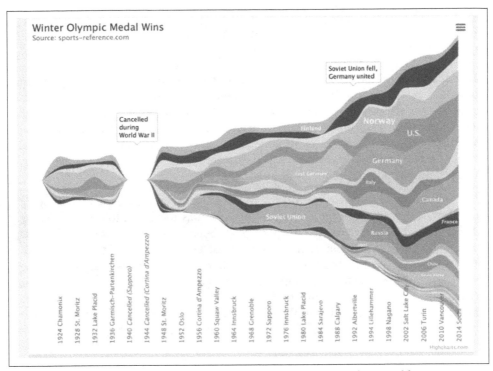

Figure 3-1. A sophisticated chart built with the Highcharts visualization library

Another concern for development teams arises when building analytics redirects resources from other development tasks. If those developers are not already specialists in data and analytics, their learning curve can be steep. And the problems of data integration, administration, and security remain.

In short, although component libraries can offer very sophisticated visual capabilities, the burden of maintaining connectivity and data management in code is likely to require too much effort in deployment for all but the simplest scenarios.

There's Always a Way

Donald Farmer

I once advised a computer gaming company that had an excellent, highly skilled development team. In fact, almost all the senior people were practiced developers who had arrived in their roles along separate paths but with a software background. They were also visual thinkers, who enjoyed working with sophisticated charts and visualizations. As a result, many of the managers, whether in marketing or product management, had built their own visual tools, connected to the corporate data lake, using component libraries.

Yet even for these sophisticated users, governing data access and security, managing versions, and applying corporate role-based rules was too much to do in code. So, rather than embedding analytics in operational applications, they chose a BI platform that could be extended with custom components. The BI platform included features for security, governance, and administration, while the component library offered the visualizations they wanted. This rather topsy-turvy way of doing things worked for them, but only because everyone from the CFO to the secretary was a developer at heart. I don't recommend it, but the story is worth telling if only to remind us that there's a solution for every scenario, if we are just innovative enough.

Enterprise Reporting Platforms

If you work in a large organization, you almost certainly have an existing enterprise reporting platform, and this may be the easiest place to start with embedded analytics. These applications are designed to provide a standardized view of business data at scale across your organization. Typically, a centralized IT team develops, maintains, and deploys the platform and applications, which helps with standardization but limits customization and agility. In fact, development and deployment cycles can end up quite extended.

Nevertheless, reports can embed quite easily into an application, typically populating an inline frame in HTML; all we must do is point to the report's address on an enterprise server. However, simplicity often comes with limited functionality. Interactions with the report are commonly limited to sorting, searching, and some simple filtering. Equally, embedding can raise all sorts of issues for reporting platforms. Reports with large numbers of records may not paginate properly within a frame, and scrolling to find records does not fit with our Orientation–Glimpsing–Examining–Deciding model from Chapter 2.

Some features of enterprise reports may prove useful in an embedded scenario. For example, when data repeats in groups, reports can be *banded* as in Figure 3-2. Be careful, however, that these experiences, intended for standalone reports, are appropriate and not distracting when embedded.

Financial summary			
Unrestricted activity	FY 2012	FY 2013	FY 2014
Unrestricted operating revenue			
Earned program	$1,181,314	$1,435,918	$1,099,321
Earned non-program	$182,851	$131,113	$152,849
Total earned revenue	$1,364,165	$1,516,626	$1,233,916
Investment revenue	$74,328	$69,174	$87,378
Contributed revenue	$1,911,793	$1,886,793	$2,576,007
Total unrestricted operating revenue	$3,349,793	$3,472,593	$3,897,301
Operating expenses			
Program	$1,979,211	$2,017,716	$2,001,304
Fundraising	$253,171	$246,655	$251,202
General and administrative	$1,283,413	$1,446,689	$1,398,314
Total operating expenses	$3,515,795	$3,711,060	$3,650,820
Net unrestricted activity: operating	-$166,002	-$238,467	$246,481
Net unrestricted activity: non-operating	$0	$0	$0
Total net unrestricted activity	-$166,002	-$238,467	$246,481
Net temporarily restricted activity	-$63,700	-$400,022	$6,949,016
Net permanently restricted activity	$0	$0	$0
Net total activity	-$229,702	-$638,489	$7,195,497

Figure 3-2. A banded report

Good scenarios for using reports include where you need to embed a standardized enterprise view in a simple format, where limited interaction is acceptable, and where data (or at least summary fields) are easily presented within a frame. Do ensure that the report is genuinely relevant to the workflow of the hosting application. Some scenarios, however, do not have an operational workflow as such. For example, reports such as that shown in Figure 3-3 can be embedded in an enterprise portal, such as Microsoft SharePoint. These reports are largely static objects; perhaps we should not think of this use case as truly *analytic*.

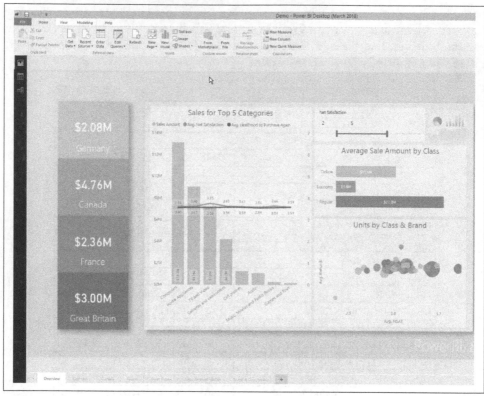

Figure 3-3. A Power BI report that can be embedded, for example, in Microsoft SharePoint

Embedding a report that does not provide the most relevant information in the right context will be at best a waste of effort and too often confusing, clumsy, and counterproductive. And reports, even when embedded, look like reports. They are mostly for reference and do not encourage new perspectives or discoveries.

Business Intelligence Applications

When we move beyond the simplest reporting and dashboard solutions, BI applications offer more in the way of customization and the ability for users to perform their own exploration and analysis. These BI platforms often include good navigation features for orientation, a wide range of visualizations for glimpsing, and powerful interactive features for examining data. However, they do require more training than simple reports to be used effectively. Several leading BI platforms also use in-memory processing, which promises great performance for even complex scenarios but may limit the use of big data in data lakes.

Having said that these applications offer more interactivity than reports, we should also point out that this flexibility comes with its own costs. The user experience, especially the navigation or selection features, may be different from the host application's. When you have one method of selecting or moving between records in the host application and another in the embedded analysis, the experience can be confusing and distracting.

You may also find the BI application has its own security model and security architecture, with the result that it may not be able to inherit permissions from the host application.

However, if the BI application is already widely deployed in your business, it may seem very convenient to embed it into a host application. In such cases, users are not learning a completely new methodology. Indeed, they may appreciate a familiar environment. If this approach is attractive, make sure you investigate whether the BI application is actually widely used and appreciated. Just being deployed is not enough. Embedding an unpopular or underused application is not a path to success!

While some BI applications can be embedded into a host application as easily as a report—using an iframe, for example—several have more advanced features for embeddability, such as dedicated container components and APIs for developers. Using an iframe is attractive if you simply want to add a few analytic features, or even specific analytic tabs, to your existing application, but using an iframe for each embedded component can badly affect performance.

Although developers may appreciate the APIs included with BI applications, too often they find the programmable or embeddable functionality limited and clumsy to work with. This can happen when the vendor develops the APIs some time after the BI application itself: in other words, when they are added on rather than built in. APIs developed in this way are often less well integrated, less reliable (being more complex to test), and less carefully defined. These APIs may also be less fully documented.

For many businesses it makes sense to reuse the work they have already put into their existing BI development. Very often what we want to embed is not a completely new report or visualization, but a version of something that is already in use elsewhere in the organization. But as we have seen, there are some limitations and compromises in this approach.

When we need to develop new solutions from scratch, or when the limitations get in the way of an optimal user experience for the host application, then it is time to look at specialized tools.

Purpose-Built Embedded Platforms

When you need to develop best-in-class embedded analytics, you will naturally look for a best-in-class platform and toolset for development.

Some vendors have created platforms designed from the ground up to be embedded and extended by developers. The APIs are an integral component of the platform architecture. In the ideal case, the vendors' own developers build the product with the same APIs external developers can use. This thorough approach avoids nearly all the difficulties of add-on APIs. At their best these APIs encapsulate the most common and most compelling functions of the system in well-documented, clear constructs that can be called simply from your own code.

Being designed from the beginning to be embedded, these platforms are also more likely to have navigation and exploration features that can be called from the hosting application with a consistent user experience. In Figure 3-4 you can see analytics fully embedded in an operational application. Indeed, it can be difficult here to tell which elements of the UX are analytic and which are operational.

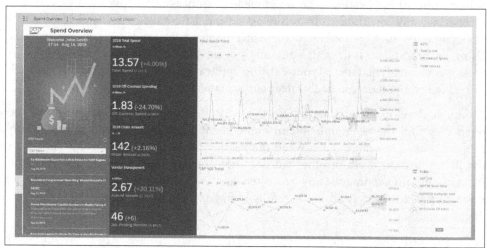

Figure 3-4. Analytics fully embedded in an operational application

A good embedded analytics platform should ship with a range of out-of-the-box functions for common scenarios. This will ensure that development and deployment are fast and reliable.

It is important for an embedded solution to integrate with the security features of the host application. We will discuss this more in Chapter 6, but for now be aware that with a good embedded platform, security integration should be straightforward.

For sure, these embedded platforms require more skills and training than a simple component library. But the completeness of their features and the power of their analytics are often worth the extra effort. These platforms should also ship with a software development kit (SDK), which should include detailed documentation, sample code and components (such as JavaScript components) for data connectivity, and custom visualizations to help developers quickly build and test an application.

Embedded Self-Service

Self-service analytics platforms are now the most popular form of business intelligence application. This approach offers business users the chance to build their own analytics with tools specifically designed for the purpose. In theory, we can then free up IT resources from dashboard development for other work, thus removing bottlenecks. Also in theory, business users can get exactly what they want without a lengthy cycle of requirements gathering and prototyping with an IT team.

In *practice*, self-service rarely works out quite so ideally. As business users create more analytic artifacts (reports, dashboards, and low-code applications), they demand more access to data, though they may lack the analytical skills to put that data to its best use. IT must provision these tools and govern the data, though IT may lack the business knowledge to support the business users' scenarios, or to challenge how they apply their analytics in practice. Also, as these analytics proliferate, system performance can degrade (business users rarely build efficient applications), and problems of availability, governance, and compliance can increase. In a self-service system, the IT team either has to run to keep up with business users or rethink its role. See the sidebar "From Gatekeepers to Shopkeepers" on page 86 for more thoughts on this dilemma.

You might expect that self-service is not practical in an embedded scenario. However, if your platform of choice has these capabilities, users can avoid a wide range of requests to IT with some simple customization. Perhaps all they need is the ability to change a visualization type. (In spite of the best efforts of designers and visualization experts, some people still prefer a pie chart!) But they may also be able to add new filters, new selections, or even completely new reports based on a current view.

Most embedded self-service scenarios, in contrast to standalone self-service platforms, do not expect business users to build everything from scratch. Instead, business users may reuse existing objects that the developer has already created, laying them out and configuring them in new ways.

However, there is one important challenge you must ensure you can address before enabling embedded self-service: upgrading customizations. If your users can create their own objects—reports, dashboards, new configurations—then, when you upgrade the application, the platform must detect and respect those customizations. Otherwise, users can lose their carefully crafted work, or the hosting application may break in unpredictable ways.

Summary

Table 3-1 summarizes the main differences among the options described in this chapter.

Table 3-1. Architectural platforms for embedded analytics

Architecture	Benefits	Weaknesses
Component libraries	• User experience can exactly match the host application.	• Every component must be customized in code. • Security and administration must be coded for each component. • Maintenance can be complicated to implement and test.
Enterprise reports	• Centrally governed. • Highly scalable. • Standardized across the enterprise.	• Long development cycle. • Restricted user options or customization. • Limited interactivity.
Business intelligence applications	• Rich palette of visualizations. • Good range of connectivity. • High performance from in-memory engines.	• User experience can be very different from the host application. • Highly interactive environment can confuse or distract users. • Security is unlikely to be integrated with the host application.
Embedded analytics platforms	• Highly customizable, even enabling some self-service. • Optimized for embedding. • Integrates with application security and administration.	• Higher cost than component libraries. • Requires more training than component libraries.

In this chapter we have looked at the common elements of an embedded solution and considered some of the advantages and disadvantages of different approaches. Some of these are so important they require a more detailed consideration, so in the following chapters we will look at data and security as elements critical to your success.

CHAPTER 4

Data for Embedded Analytics

One of the first questions to ask when building an analytics solution that will be embedded inside an operational application is where the data will come from. The answer is not always simple. The data will not necessarily come from the operational application itself. In fact, very often you'll want to complement or augment the application with insights from other systems.

To do so, you'll have to consider three things for each data source that you wish to use:

- Where does the data come from? Which system has the best data to support your decisions, or to support the application that you are enhancing?

- How will you connect to that data? There are different ways of connecting (even to the same data source), which may be more or less appropriate for the scenario at hand.

- How will you manage and govern the connectivity, security, and performance of the connection to that data source?

In this chapter, we'll look at several different data sources that can be useful for embedded analytics and consider those questions.

CSV and Other Text Files

There are few data sources as simple—in theory—as a text file of data. Text files are found in almost every business in some scenario, because they have some great advantages. For one thing, they are widely supported by data analysis tools ranging from the simplest spreadsheet to the most advanced data science workbench. Comma-separated values (CSV) files are equally well supported as an export format.

Connecting to a CSV file typically only involves having read permissions to access the folder in which it is stored. So, for many situations, they are a convenient solution.

This convenience comes at a cost, however:

Security

The only security mechanism for CSV files is to protect access to the folders in which they are stored. There is no support for row or column protection. It is important, therefore, that if you are using CSV files as a source they must be exported with the strictest security and privacy controls in place. Do not save sensitive data in these files.

Performance

Most data movement tools, such as extract, transform, load (ETL) applications for data warehouses, are optimized in some way for text files, especially for reading or writing data in bulk. These optimizations often take the form of read and write buffers that load data into memory for parsing. BI tools rarely have these optimizations in place. They will read text files easily, but performance is likely to be poor compared to a native application driver.

Parsing

Not all text files are CSV files. Some are delimited by tab characters, some by pipe or vertical bar characters. Highly customized delimiters are rare—and ironically, ASCII control codes, intended to be a standard, are rarer still—but you may encounter them. Numerous issues can arise with numbers, such as the use of different decimal separators (some countries use commas) or unusual placement of the thousands separator (such as in the Indian numbering system, which uses lakhs and crores). If your analytics environment does not support these characteristics, you will need to ensure that your data export process renders the text files in an easily readable format.

Metadata

With CSV files, if we only read the data in the file, we do not get metadata about when it was last updated. Sometimes, for example in finance, these files are manually updated every week or month when the department has all the data available. If we open the file manually in a spreadsheet, we may get some information embedded in the filename, in some header cells, or in an embedded info table in the file. But if we just read in the data with a semi-automated process, that metadata is lost. Also, unlike a database table, text files have a higher risk of human errors because numbers can just be typed in without validation.

Operational Data Sources

An *operational data source* is simply the location where an operational application's data is stored. All modern applications, to some extent, create, store, and manage data. For example, an application for processing orders generates the data for each order and perhaps links data for each customer. That will need to be persisted somewhere. Operational data sources focus on integrating that data in such a way that the performance of the application is maximized and the integrity of the application is ensured. In many cases, the ease of use, especially the responsiveness of the application, is enhanced by having a robust data store that can persist large volumes of data for recordkeeping with good performance.

Many applications use very simple structures for operational data sources. For example, many use an underlying operational database. Developers are typically familiar with connectivity to that database and with the table structure, because they work with the operational application on a daily basis. And because you're connecting directly to your operational data source, the consistency of the data is pretty much guaranteed.

Sometimes, you may use a copy of the operational source. For example, you may take advantage of a technology such as replication. The advantage of that for a developer is that the work they do with analytics doesn't affect the operational application itself. So, for example, you could extract all the records for an individual customer, aggregate them to do some analysis, and then present that to the operator. You don't have to look up all the details in the original database because you're using a replicated copy, which improves performance and preserves the consistency of the original data source.

As we said, operational data structures are optimized for efficiency and integrity. But the implication of this is that they are *not* optimized for analytics. In practice, the joins between tables in a highly normalized database can be very complex and tricky to navigate, and often don't provide the best performance for analysis. In such cases, trying to execute analytics over these tables becomes an extra load on the database. Replication can help with that, but if replication has too much latency, you may find discontinuity between operations and analytics: the order just placed on the phone doesn't show up in the report.

However, *connectivity* to the operational data source is typically simple, because your operational application is already connected to it. If the data source is a replicated version of the operational data source, connectivity is only slightly different, requiring a distinct connection string but no other changes.

The situation does get a little more difficult if we are trying to combine two operational systems: one in which we are performing operations and one from which we are sourcing data to enhance the analytics.

You may have a purchase management system that handles orders and invoices and various aspects of the order-to-delivery process. The customer data may be in a different application, such as a customer relationship management (CRM) system or a financial system. Bringing those two together involves embedding one within the other, but they're both operational systems and therefore not particularly optimized for analytics.

For any operational system, there are typically two ways to connect: through a bulk connector or through an API. A *bulk connector* is optimized for extracting a large amount of data. An example of this is connecting with OLE DB or JDBC to the operational database underlying the application. With such a connector, you can ask for a full table of information, or for many tables at a time, and you can probably issue a query against it and return a result set, which may be small or large. That kind of connectivity can be useful for analytics because typically we're looking at larger volumes of data to analyze.

The other way to connect to operational systems is through an API (if that's supported). Web developers will be familiar with this, because most of the connectivity between web applications involves API calls. However, APIs are typically not designed for returning large volumes of data: often only single records or the answer to a simple query and the result set may be returned as an XML document rather than as a flat table. Even worse, the limitations on data volume in an API call can mean the developer has to page through the data, making several API calls to slowly build the full result set.

As a result, we have to be careful in choosing the kind of connectivity that we want to use for analytics. It will not always be the case that an OLE DB connector is the best. Many of them are very simple and performance may not be good. Equally, it will not always be the case that an API is inappropriate. Some APIs *do* have calls that enable bulk data extraction. In other words, we have to know our system pretty well to understand the volume of data we are trying to extract, the characteristics of the source system, and the workload we ask it to perform.

One way of working with operational data sources is to add new objects—views and aggregation tables—to the database schema. Aggregation tables and views are both database objects used in database design to organize and present data in a useful way.

Aggregation tables contain summarized data. They can be precalculated and stored in the database to improve query performance and reduce the amount of time required to generate reports. *Views*, on the other hand, are virtual tables created by combining data from one or more existing tables in the database. Views can simplify complex queries and provide a simplified, organized view of the data for end users.

Analytic Data Sources

In this section, we discuss the three types of data sources we might consider as analytic: data warehouses, in-memory engines, and data lakes.

Data Warehouses

The most common analytic data source is the *data warehouse*, an architecture specifically intended to enable data analysis. Its data is denormalized to make it simple to query and to improve the performance of large analytic queries. The architecture is designed to integrate data from multiple data sources so that work does not need to be repeated. Most importantly, the data warehouse represents not just a data structure, but a business model. That is to say, it is a logical representation of how a business operates.

A data warehouse will have a *customer dimension* that represents how the business thinks about its customers, and a *geography dimension* that represents how the business thinks about its divisions, offices, and stores or factories. A data warehouse nearly always includes a *time dimension* that represents the calendars, working days, holidays, and seasonal divisions relevant to the business. It may include a *personnel dimension*, which reflects the structure of the company's hierarchy. All of these predesigned and prepopulated dimensions make analytic queries very simple for the developer. Even better, the data warehouse should be optimized for analytic performance.

In fact, a data warehouse—or its simpler, more focused cousin, the data mart—is the primary source for many business intelligence systems and an excellent source of data for embedded analytics.

But not every enterprise, and certainly not every small or medium-sized business, has a data warehouse. Even those enterprises that do have a data warehouse may not want to make it available for operational applications, because in some cases the warehouse is focused on management, financial, or tax reporting: that is, mission-critical business analysis, which may be sensitive or governed in such a way that the business does not wish to make the data directly available to other systems.

Sometimes, we can work around that by creating downstream replications of specific subject areas and even the answers to specific queries that we use regularly.

In-Memory Engines

The data warehouse technology with which we are familiar has been with us since the 1990s. Around 2005, another technology started to appear that has many of the advantages of a data warehouse but offers greater performance and flexibility and has advantages for both large and small businesses. This is the *in-memory engine*, which takes advantage of the very high performance of memory as compared to disk for performing complex queries. With 64-bit systems (and cheap memory chips) emerging in the mid-2000s, companies could perform analysis on a desktop that previously had only been possible on the largest corporate systems.

Building on these desktop capabilities, in-memory technologies are very popular in self-service business intelligence and are the key to the performance and flexibility of many of the most popular self-service applications, such as Microsoft Power BI, Salesforce Tableau, and Qlik. In the past, self-service applications were very self-contained and focused on their own analytic capabilities. Their connectivity to other systems was entirely focused on extracting data into their own memory space, and developers didn't think very much about how they would share that data with other systems. However, many of the in-memory BI applications available today enable embedding. So, more often than not, it's possible to take a chart from a BI tool and embed it inside an operational application. This has benefits for developers in terms of familiarity, performance, and simplicity, but there are some limitations because the systems are often not designed from the start to be embedded. Rather, the embedding ability (and the APIs) may be afterthoughts, which have been added later. Nevertheless, for developers familiar with these systems, and where the systems are already deployed in the business or in the enterprise, it's a very attractive proposition to reuse this functionality and embed it inside operational applications. This scenario is often well supported by the tools and their user communities, and it's an option that is well worth considering.

Data Lakes

Like the data warehouse, the *data lake* architecture (and, in its more modern incarnation, the *data lakehouse*) is focused on the storage of large volumes of data, which are made available for purposes such as data science and, to some extent, analytics.

Unlike the data warehouse, the data lake does not have a built-in business model—that is, a logical semantic architecture that represents how the business thinks about itself, with rules, well-defined processes for governance, or easily navigated data structures. In fact, the data lake is intended to store data in its most raw format *without* any processing. This is a great advantage for data scientists, who often want to see data in its native state, because they can use that raw data to do more detailed and more complex analyses than they could if the data had already been cleaned up and built into a data model for reporting.

In the data lake, the data scientist can see all the raw detail, with all its errors and complexities. But the business user may find it very difficult to integrate and transform data in the lake as they need it.

Data Integration Pipelines

Another source of data for an embedded system may be the output of a *data integration pipeline*. That is to say, rather than reading data from a table in an in-memory system or a data warehouse or operational database, the data is read from a pipeline running in a data science environment. The pipeline may perform numerous operations of integration, cleansing, and preparation on the data, from whatever source it comes. This is a popular scenario for data science. However, it is of limited use for embedded analytics, because the pipeline is more dynamic and more volatile, only delivering data while it is running, which makes the process more fragile and more difficult to govern than a data warehouse or an in-memory system.

A scenario where this is popular and useful is when data is continuously changing, referred to as *streaming data*. This could include data from machines, such as automated lathes in manufacturing, or from an ecommerce ordering system where hundreds of orders may be placed every minute, or from environmental sensors.

In such cases, the analytic scenario is somewhat different and performance is still a consideration. An application offering streaming analytics must include methodologies for handling interruptions to the stream. In addition, it must be able to display changing values without users having to manually refresh the display. Finally, methodologies for governance and security may be different from the analytic governance that we're used to.

Writing Back to Sources

A final point has to be made about the handling of data in embedded analytics. We have been talking so far about data *extracted* from source systems and presented in the embedded analytics environment purely for the purposes of information and augmentation. This is a read-only scenario. However, there may be times when we want to make changes to the analytic system from within the embedded application—what we call *write-back*.

Write-back is often used for planning and simulation applications, where we want to insert numbers that represent future estimates of sales or staffing or growth, or whatever the parameters are that we are planning around. It is relatively unusual for systems designed for analysis, such as a data warehouse, to enable direct write-back. Such systems are too concerned with data integrity, data history, and compliance to allow ad hoc changes. But often they will allow write-back to special tables, which can be set up as parameter tables specifically for the purpose.

Summary

We have seen that data can be sourced for embedded analytics from many different kinds of systems: operational, analytic, and streaming. There is no one best solution for a typical embedded scenario, but it is fair to say that most developers of embedded applications will start with a simple data warehouse or data mart scenario if that already exists within their organization.

Table 4-1 summarizes some of the benefits and weaknesses of the approaches we have discussed.

Table 4-1. Data sources for embedded analytics

Data source	Benefits	Weaknesses
CSV files	• Widely supported, often human readable.	• No security mechanism. • May be difficult to parse. • Performance may be poor. • Fragile to user errors.
Operational database	• Developers are familiar with the connectivity and table structure. • Because you are connecting to operational data, consistency is guaranteed. • If replication is available, you may use a copy of the operational system for analytics.	• Operational table structures are optimized for efficient transactions, not for analytics. Joins can be complex. • Analytics is an extra load on the database and can affect performance, although replication can help.
Views and aggregate tables	• Analytic queries are simplified because the joins were developed in advance. • Filtering is simple. • You can apply role-based access rules simply or build them into the view. (Like the secured views of some cloud data warehouses.) • Aggregating data in advance improves performance.	• Response time may be slow if the underlying joins are complex. • Views and aggregate tables must be maintained separately from operational tables: another burden for administrators. • Aggregate tables must be updated, often using triggers. Updates have to be carefully scheduled or they will affect the performance of the operational system.
Data mart or data warehouse	• High performance, as the architecture and schema are optimized for analytic queries. • Simple to integrate with BI and analytics tools, as the schema is designed for analysis. • Load on the transactional source system is reduced.	• Loading the data warehouse using ETL is a specialized practice. • The load and refresh cycle of the warehouse (often scheduled to run overnight) may be too slow for analytics embedded in an operational application. • Changing the schema can be complex, requiring a lengthy process of specifying, implementing, and testing.
In-memory engine	• Very high performance. • Should be closely integrated with the embedded analytics environment.	• Support for writing back to the database is often limited. • Data updates may be occasional and often require full, rather than incremental, updates.

Data source	Benefits	Weaknesses
Data lake	• If using a data lakehouse architecture, you will find many of the same benefits as a data warehouse. • Data is generally stored in its native format, which can be good for predictive analytics. • Data may be continuously updated.	• If not using a lakehouse architecture, you may find performance for business intelligence poor because so much transformation is required to conform and shape data. • Data lakes are generally shared with data scientists, data engineers, and analysts. Security can be a concern. • The use of raw data increases the risk of users seeing different variations of the same data because the data has not been validated to the same extent as in a data warehouse or mart.

In general, we recommend starting with a data mart or data warehouse connection if this already exists in your organization's architecture. You'll find it gives the best balance of accessibility, performance, and governance for your needs. A data lake or lakehouse, if well managed, offers some similar advantages. However, if you don't already have a formal data warehouse or lakehouse in place, it is a significant effort to build one and likely beyond the scope of your embedded analytics project on its own.

In this case, you may find it practical to start with views and aggregate tables, defined for your purposes and hosted within the operational database. The administrator can provision access and ensure security and good governance, performance should be acceptable, and data access should be possible with a suitable driver.

Having reviewed the data sources that are available, in the next chapter we'll consider the different types of embeddable objects and how we can integrate them visually with applications for the most effective support.

CHAPTER 5

Embedding Analytics Objects

Now that we've discussed the potential data sources that can power embedded analytics solutions, we can consider the actual *objects* that we can embed. In this chapter, we'll talk about the various types of analytics objects, how users and consumers interact with them, and what considerations—technical and otherwise—should be evaluated when planning, developing, and implementing embedded solutions.

We'll explore the ways in which embedded objects can be visually integrated into third-party applications to provide a seamless experience for end users, and we will also cover specific technical processes that extend functionality and allow embedded solutions to integrate with other enterprise resource planning (ERP), CRM, and communication platforms.

 In this chapter, we're being deliberately broad by using the term "object" to refer to any analytical element, component, or content embedded within a host application, whether it's served from within the host application itself or from an external source or application.

What Can We Embed?

It's worth outlining some ways to categorize the types of analytics objects that can be embedded in any solution. First, we should remind ourselves that embedded analytics isn't just about integrating analytics objects, but also analytical *capabilities*. These capabilities—like natural language generation (NLG), for example—help end users make better decisions in the same way as more typical embedded objects like charts and graphs, but often rely on very different technical approaches. Second, while categorizing objects in this way is useful, bear in mind that truly effective embedded analytics solutions will often combine these capabilities to provide better accessibility and encourage adoption by less technical users.

Let's look at some examples.

Key Performance Indicators

From an analytics standpoint, *key performance indicator* (KPI) is one of the most common terms you'll hear when dealing with embedded analytics. In simple terms, it represents a measurable value that evaluates progress toward a previously agreed objective, like a sales target, response time, or quarterly revenue. Although KPIs can be considered as a type of data visualization (static or otherwise), we'd encourage you to consider them as a distinct type of object, for a couple of reasons:

- They're almost always *highly aggregated* measures or give a very simple visual indication of what's happening to an aggregated measure. Is this figure positive or negative? Are sales up or down? This is particularly important in the context of embedded analytics, where quickly giving end users some level of directional insight means they can "stay in the flow" without spending a long time interacting with or interpreting complex charts.

- The nature of KPIs means that they are a powerful way of presenting a lot of high-level insight in a relatively small area. Again, this is useful for embedded use cases, where room on the page or within an application may be given over to other content, not just analytics.

Figure 5-1 illustrates a typical use of KPIs to summarize the performance of three metrics. Note that KPIs are often augmented by other indicative objects to add some context. In this case, our SALES YTD KPI shows us an aggregated sales value along with the change in that value (expressed as a value and a percentage change) compared with the same period a year ago. There's also a color-coded indicator to help us quickly see if the change is an increase or decrease. This approach builds on the basic idea of a single-metric KPI and starts to use some more complex data visualization techniques.

Figure 5-1. A section of a dashboard illustrating various KPIs

Data Visualizations

Humans are pattern recognition machines. Interpreting data visually gives us less cognitive work to do, and our brains are better suited to it. We also tend to process visual information in very predictable and consistent ways, so it makes sense that data visualizations are the mainstay of any embedded analytics solution.

There are thousands of resources, books, and websites out there devoted to the topic of data visualization (as of the time of writing, Amazon returns more than seven thousand results for the term), which go into exhaustive detail about the history, creation, and interpretation of charts and graphs. However, for our purposes, let's summarize some key types of data visualization objects you'll see in embedded analytics solutions by thinking about what they're *for*, as well as what they look like.

Column and bar charts, shown in Figure 5-2, are most often used to compare the size (or magnitude) of things, like total sales across regions.

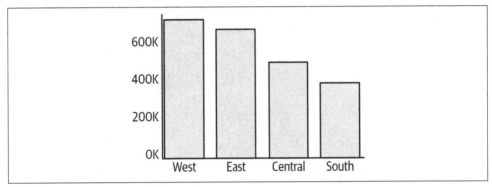

Figure 5-2. An example of a bar chart

Figure 5-3 shows a histogram. They're often used to show how frequently things happen and are the standard way to show statistical distributions, like the breakdown of a population by age category.

Line charts, like the one shown in Figure 5-4, and their derivatives (area charts, step charts, etc.) are used to show how something changes over time, like daily call volumes in a call center. Line charts are often the basis for trend charts.

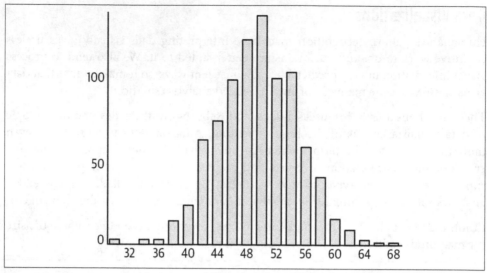

Figure 5-3. An example of a histogram

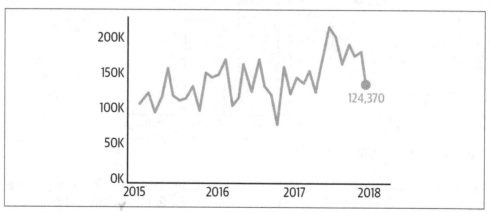

Figure 5-4. An example of a line chart

Gantt charts, like the one shown in Figure 5-5, are of relevance to embedded solutions where the user is already working in an ERP or CRM application. They are useful for visualizing the duration and relationship of things over time, like tasks in a project.

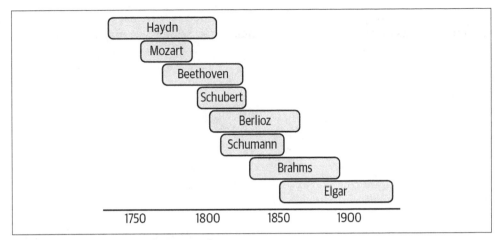

Figure 5-5. An example of a Gantt chart

Stacked bar charts, like the example in Figure 5-6, are often used to show the relationship of part-to-whole data, like the breakdown of budget spending by category. The most common (and controversial) type of part-to-whole data visualization most people are familiar with is the pie chart.

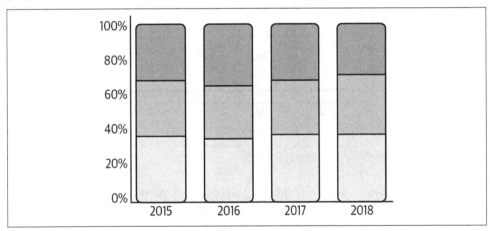

Figure 5-6. An example of a stacked bar chart

Spatial charts, like the example in Figure 5-7, are used to visualize data in relation to specific locations or geographic areas, like plotting locations on a map expecting rain.

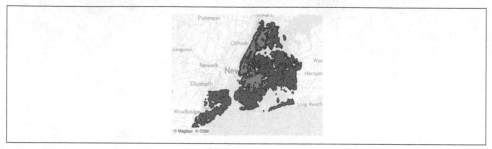

Figure 5-7. An example of a spatial chart

Scatter plots, like the example in Figure 5-8, are used to show the relationship between two variables, like the correlation between age and shoe size.

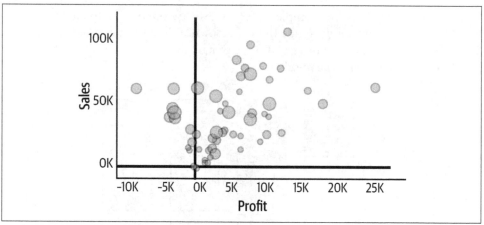

Figure 5-8. An example of a scatter plot

Naturally, many other chart and graph derivatives and combinations exist, along with more esoteric chart types like radar charts, Isotypes, Sankey diagrams, and chord charts—all of which have specific use cases.

These chart types can be very powerful at bringing insight to end users, but I'd advise anyone stepping into the world of data visualization to remember that a chart or graph is only as effective as a viewer's ability to understand it—or indeed *interact* with it, something we'll go into more detail about later.

Tabular Data

What do we mean by "tabular"? As an all-encompassing definition, we can start with "data presented in a table," which for most of us means a spreadsheet, like an Excel document or a Google Sheet. As mentioned in previous chapters, spreadsheets remain an executive tool of choice, and they're the most common and fundamental way that users encounter analytical content within applications.

Let's look at a few examples.

Figure 5-9 is a great example of a summarized, tabular analytics object embedded in a website, showing summarized data about COVID vaccination statuses in various Australian jurisdictions. As with our KPI example, this table also includes data visualization techniques (color-coded heatmapping computed at the column level) to help readers identify the highest and lowest values.

Jurisdiction	One dose	Two doses	Three doses	Four doses
AUS	86.98	84.4	54.98	17.45
NSW	86.95	84.64	53.55	17.85
VIC	88.2	85.69	57.36	16.92
QLD	81.6	79.14	46.84	16.64
WA	85.43	82.74	62.3	16.38
SA	84.92	82.1	56.34	19.57
TAS	87.34	84.72	56.86	21.29
ACT	89.65	87.35	61.47	20.3
NT	79.04	75.1	53.18	8.46

Figure 5-9. Tabular analytics object with color-coded heatmapping (source: CovidLive.com.au)

You're also highly likely to encounter tabular objects in CRM and ERP systems, like what's shown in Figure 5-10: an example of a Salesforce page that summarizes yearly sales performance figures. Note that there's a high level of precision for the aggregated figures in the bottom section. Whether or not this is useful to the viewer is a decision you need to make when using any kind of aggregated values shown in tabular format.

	Jan 2020	Feb 2020	Mar 2020	Apr 2020	May 2020	Jun 2020
Finance and transactions						
Orders value	2409	3670	3345	1450	2334	6000
Operational Exp.	0.07	0.03	0.05	0.25	0.04	0.012
Cashback value	240	367	335	145	233	600
Aggregated data						
Mid Market value	6.5687	5.7896	5.2656	6.5687	7.5687	8.5687
Market growth	0.005	-0.001	0.001	-0.015	-0.107	-0.096

Figure 5-10. Section of a page in a CRM system

Dynamic Text and NLG Content

As the capabilities of data and analytics applications continue to increase, text-based content is often used to augment embedded analytics and present insights in context for users to read without needing to interpret data visualizations. Consider the following example:

> **In-store** is the top-performing sales category, contributing **$131,092** to the total sales in the US over the last **12** months. This represents a **6% increase** over the same period last year.

Here, static (predetermined) text is augmented with four dynamic (data-driven) fields that update based on a data source. The advantage of this approach is that it requires low cognitive effort to interpret the data and the text can be tightly integrated with other nonanalytical content in an embedded solution. Depending on the way this is visually structured, users may not even be aware they're interpreting analytical data at all—potentially an impressive achievement.

Going beyond dynamic text, NLG technology uses machine learning techniques and computation linguistics to produce written text from data sources without the need to predetermine structure or syntax. As of the time of writing, this fast-evolving technology is often presented as a complementary technology alongside many of the leading data visualization tools, both to add value to traditional data visualization dashboards for end users and as an aid to statistical analysis, allowing users with appropriate knowledge to quickly identify significant trends and outliers.

In the following example, all the text has been generated by an NLG system, including the grammatical structure and presentation of language as well as the data-driven metrics. If well configured and carefully deployed, you can imagine how powerful this kind of approach can be, and how much time it can potentially save, within embedded analytics solutions:

Last year's Technology orders shipped on time or early 75% of the time. Strong performance in Standard Class Shipping, where 90% of orders shipped on time or early, is a possible explanation for this good shipping year. The South Region is another likely reason, as 81% of these orders shipped on time or early.

Adding Interactivity

As we have mentioned already, embedded analytics isn't just about integrating analytics objects, but also analytical capabilities. NLG is a great example of embedding an analytical capability, but it's not something immediately obvious to an end user. One of the most effective ways to provide additional capability is to embed objects that users can interact with.

Interaction Examples

When we talk about interacting with analytics objects, we simply mean providing some element of human input: clicking a button, dragging a scroll bar, entering a value into a search box. Here are some examples:

- *Hovering* over an object to reveal some additional or contextual detail about a data point on a chart. Tool tips are the most common examples of this, but this technique can also be used to trigger other actions, like highlighting related objects or areas on other charts.

- *Selecting* data points on a chart in order to filter related objects on other charts. Selections on data visualizations can often be made using the same mechanisms used in popular application interfaces—dragging, multiple selections, etc.

- *Drilling into* (or "down" or "through") a single element in a data visualization in order to expand the constituent elements. While driven by a selection, this is an extremely common technique in embedded analytics solutions to allow users to move from KPIs or highly aggregated objects into more granular or row-level views for more detailed analysis.

- *Navigation* using traditional methods like tabs, menu links, icons, etc. This is another common interaction technique used to allow users to move through a sequence of data visualizations, perhaps embedded in a single page.

Of course, the expectation is that whatever you're interacting with updates quickly to show the result of your input and, crucially, adds some additional capability or value to the embedded object(s). However, it's entirely possible to use lots of complex interaction techniques and end up with a complicated, unintuitive, and meaningless analytic experience. Let's look at an imaginary example that makes good use of some of these techniques.

In Figure 5-11, the embedded object (a dashboard) is displayed as a menu option, tightly integrated within a CRM system. The user has access to other areas of the CRM system with a single click, and the analytics content in this section has been created with a visual style that matches the rest of the system.

Figure 5-11. An interactive dashboard embedded in a CRM system

Within the dashboard itself, we're making use of several techniques we've already touched on. The user can *hover* over a data point in the bar chart to see a tool tip containing some more detailed information, they can *click* on a bar to filter the details in the grid, and they can *apply custom settings* that will affect the way the KPIs are calculated. The fact that this is a Summary dashboard is clearly indicated with navigation buttons, and the user can *navigate* to additional dashboards as needed.

Interaction as a Value-Add

It's also useful to think about interactivity from a *product experience* perspective, putting yourself in the position of an end user and thinking critically about the actual use case. Will users *want* to interact with visualizations? Will they *need* to interact to get actionable insights, or is a simpler method more appropriate?

Many embedded analytics solutions use interactivity as a unique selling point (USP) to support higher-cost access for users and consumers. You can easily imagine a free bronze plan that provides access to a limited number of noninteractive objects, versus a paid gold plan that provides access to a broader range of fully interactive objects.

Designing a system that offers a great experience to its users applies to embedded analytics solutions, just like every other user interface.

Technical Considerations

For interactive analytics to provide value, interaction response times must be fast. In a perfect world, to create the illusion that a user is directly manipulating something on a screen, a response time of less than 0.2 seconds (200 ms) is required. This might seem ambitious, but bear in mind that common interactions with preloaded objects like buttons, drop-down lists, and link behaviors on a typical website are usually within this range.

However, in the context of embedded analytics we might need to lower our expectations. It's true that many analytics tools have "instant" responses to user interactions for native features like tool tips, drop-down filters, and selections. But if the interaction generates a query to the underlying data source (or otherwise requires new data to be loaded and rendered), there will be a delay, and it's likely to be longer than 200 ms. So, when planning an embedded analytics solution, you should do the following:

Consider the impact that infrastructure and solution design might have on response times.

Optimized, denormalized data extracted from your data mart or data warehouse (which lives close to your analytics solution) *may* perform faster than a live connection to a table hosted in a cloud data warehouse. Similarly, optimizing and right-sizing hardware for analytical workloads can yield great results.

Understand the caching model that analytics products use and how it may impact your solution.

Most database, data warehouse, and data lake products have complex and sophisticated query and result caching capabilities, which can often be used in conjunction with data visualization product caching to only generate new queries or page loads when it's necessary, thus reducing response time to an absolute minimum.

Define upper and lower bounds for interaction response and monitor them.

Knowing what "good" looks like leads to efficient optimization and management. If a 5-second response time is likely to be sufficient for your use case, then efforts can be targeted at only the worst-performing objects, pages, and visualizations.

Test the general performance of embedded content and the impact that concurrent users have on your solution.

Concurrency can be complex to define, but having some understanding of how response times are affected when a large number of users simultaneously interact with the same object(s) can be very useful, especially when scaling embedded analytics solutions.

In general, having a good grasp of the technical architecture of any planned solution will likely surface many of these considerations during evaluation.

Embedding Objects with iframes

So how do we embed analytics objects in our target application or web page? Let's explore one of the most common methods used by almost every analytics platform that supports embedding of visualizations: the iframe.

 Note that we're talking about *true* embedding here—i.e., embedding content from a third-party source (like a data visualization tool) in a target application or website (like a CRM or ERP platform), be it accessed via a browser or mobile application. Clearly, some analytics objects may appear to be embedded in a target application, when in fact they're actually integrated within the application itself.

Embedded analytics solutions, where the content or object being embedded is being served from a different system than that of the page it's embedded into, will almost always use an iframe to do the embedding.

We've made mention of these already in previous chapters. An *iframe* is a standard HTML element that can be used to load another web page within the parent page. Most popular data visualization applications have features that allow content to be embedded within iframes, either directly using URLs, or by invoking APIs to request content. This methodology can also be used in mobile apps using WebView components (*https://oreil.ly/xOtrD*).

Here's a simple example of an HTML page with an embedded iframe:

```
<h1>Here's a web page in an ERP system</h1>
<p>This content is part of the ERP system</p>
<iframe src="https://en.wikipedia.org/..." width="100%" height="300"></iframe>
<p>This content is also part of the ERP system</p>
```

In Figure 5-12, we've applied a little styling to our HTML using CSS for clarity. Everything within the red box is content we've loaded into the iframe—in this case, the Wikipedia home page. At a high level, this is exactly how embedded analytics objects are embedded in target systems.

Figure 5-12. An example of an iframe embedded in a web page

Using iframes to Our Advantage

One of the key things to consider is that when an analytics object is embedded, the end user experience is likely to be much more customizable, which is a great advantage for usability. Here are the benefits of doing this:

- Content to help users understand how to use the embedded content, such as FAQs, user guides, and tips, can be displayed alongside or in context with the embedded objects.

- Narrative content explaining interesting conclusions or insights derived from the embedded objects can be tightly integrated in an editorial fashion. Many major news outlets use this approach to support data-driven editorial content.

- Branding can be applied *around* the embedded objects to further improve the look and feel of the solution. If you're embedding a data visualization, it's entirely possible that the title and description of the content can live outside the iframe, on the parent page, and be formatted separately.

These are only basic possibilities. We'll talk more about the potential look and feel and user experience of embedded solutions later in this chapter.

Cross-Domain Limitations

Most modern web browsers have security mechanisms that restrict how resources from one origin (the web page you're browsing) can interact with resources from another origin (such as a visualization from your reporting platform displayed in an iframe on that page). The principle behind this mechanism is sound: you don't want a random website running some suspicious JavaScript code against your webmail in an embedded iframe (loaded without your consent). This security mechanism is specifically designed to prevent the "cross-origin" content from loading in the first place.

Why is this a problem for embedded solutions? In many cases, the reporting platform that serves up analytics objects may not be from the same origin as the website or app you want to embed them in.

The specifics about exactly what constitutes a different origin are beyond the scope of this book, but for our purposes we might consider a simple example where your website at *http://my.business.com* has analytics objects from *https://mi.reporting.com* embedded in it. In many browsers, this would constitute a different origin because the embedded content is not only from a different *host*, but it's also being served from a different *protocol* (HTTPS instead of HTTP).

Fortunately, there are ways to resolve cross-origin challenges, such as ensuring that both domains are explicitly trusted, or using methods like cross-origin resource sharing (CORS) (*https://oreil.ly/gNzcG*) to specify which additional origins should be permitted to load resources.

Current Embedded Analytics Trends

Embedded analytics solutions are at the heart of many data monetization products and are becoming increasingly sophisticated as organizations take advantage of software as a service (SaaS) products and other cloud services. This rapidly innovating sector has generated some interesting trends and consolidation patterns.

Using Embedded Analytics to Share Data

Many embedded analytics products are designed around the concept of self-service, which we've touched upon in previous chapters. However, it's often inevitable that such products need to allow users to select, export, and download data for other uses. In these cases, embedded objects are often used as *selection mechanisms* to identify and filter a selection of data to be exported.

As an example, consider a user drawing a selection over a map to build a selection of zip codes. In this case, the user is limited in their selection by the interactivity features in the visualization, but more sophisticated methods are available. With appropriate user authentication and authorization, it's entirely possible to allow users to write data manipulation language (DML) statements in SQL to select whatever they want from the underlying data source *alongside* the embedded options that use the same data. This is potentially a very powerful value-added proposition for an embedded solution.

Transformative Best-Practice Visualization

While adding more sophisticated features to an embedded analytics solution undeniably adds value, observing best practices for the data visualization itself is often overlooked as a way to differentiate the product. What do we mean by this? Here are some examples:

- Using the most appropriate type of visualization for the data
- Avoiding misrepresentation of data, like truncating axes to exaggerate comparative dimensions
- Careful application of color schemes, spacing, and typography

Observing these principles will make your product easier to use and more engaging for users.

The Look and Feel of Embedded Experiences

This is where the capabilities of the tool you're using to build analytics objects really come into play. Many data visualization tools are highly customizable and allow the user to build interactive experiences that are more akin to "dynamic infographics": very tightly integrated into the target system, augmented with narrative and imagery, and behaving more like an application than a traditional dashboard.

For inspiration, see Tableau's public website (*https://oreil.ly/smCIm*), which showcases some of the best examples of dynamic and interactive visualizations created using the tool.

Putting It All Together

We've talked about the types of analytics objects you can embed and how capabilities and value can be added by considering some of the human and technical aspects of embedded analytics solutions. Now let's think about what we've learned in relation to some real-world use cases.

Embedding Workflow

A core principle of embedded analytics is keeping users "in the flow" when making decisions informed by data. The fact that the analytics object is *in* the tool you're already using means you don't have to *leave* the tool, which certainly helps. But as we've discussed, the nature of the visualization, how fast it reacts, and how effective it is for the user are all significant factors.

This means it's important to think about the context of that workflow. Where has the user been before they get to see the embedded content? What will they do once they've interacted with it? How can the embedded objects drive upstream and downstream processes that might be integral to the "flow" we keep talking about?

A Typical Reporting Automation Workflow

Let's consider an example of a basic reporting workflow. A finance team needs to gather data to provide a monthly report and requires the involvement of the IT/database team to do so. Once they've got the data they need, they create a document (or update a preexisting one), and provide that to the management team to use as a decision-making tool.

What do we get with this process? Delays while different teams are involved, repetition of effort, potential for error, unmanaged proliferation of content, and potential security problems, too. This is a suboptimal pattern that's probably happening in thousands of organizations right now.

Figure 5-13 illustrates this convoluted, multidependency process as it might apply in a typical organization. This is often the first real-world use case that gets addressed with embedded analytics.

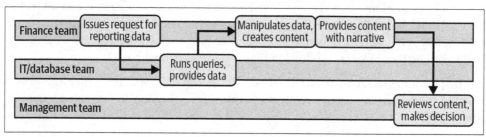

Figure 5-13. An example of a resource-intensive and costly analytics workflow

When we incorporate an embedded analytics workflow, as shown in Figure 5-14, the analytics content is integrated into an organization-wide "portal," where analytics objects are driven by data from the organization's finance database and only accessible to the management team. A given manager need only log in, review, and interact with the analytics object (a dashboard, for example) to make an informed decision.

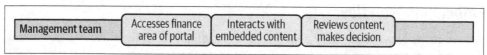

Figure 5-14. Using embedded analytics to accelerate time to insight

The contrast is obvious; there is a single report, which doesn't need to be updated by anybody. The data is accurate, access to it is tightly controlled, and the reporting content is immediately available. In fact, the finance and IT/database teams are not involved at all.

The potential time and cost savings realized by using embedded analytics in this way are nontrivial.

Using Embedded Analytics to Power Prescriptive Analytics

Prescriptive analytics is the term used to describe an analytics model where the solution specifically describes the actions needed to achieve a particular outcome. It sounds simple but often involves a lot of complexity, not least because most prescriptive analytics techniques involve presenting nontechnical users with the results of machine learning processes, which is not an easy feat to accomplish.

When embedded analytics solutions are implemented successfully, it becomes possible to integrate prescriptive analytics processes to provide a seamless experience for end users. Here's an example:

1. A sales manager accesses an embedded chart in their CRM system indicating that their sales figures are surprisingly low for the current quarter. They contemplate addressing the problem with the sales team.

2. A machine learning model, which has been trained on historical sales figures over the last five years, determines that to meet the current targets the best option would be to focus efforts on reducing the prices of three specific product categories that have historically generated strong sales, with appropriate discounts applied.

3. The specific discount percentages are determined for each product category, and the recommendation is shown alongside the embedded chart in the CRM system as the optimal way to address the poor sales performance.

This is truly closing the loop. Rather than the team addressing the issue by using intuition and guesswork, the sales manager can issue a single, statistically supported directive: *discount these three product lines and we'll be back in business.*

 It's worth noting that prescriptive analytics is rarely deployed effectively due to the complexity of the processes involved and the requirement for advanced analytics and data science and machine learning (DSML), the use of which often requires highly skilled data scientists or analytics engineers. As ever, software is increasingly democratizing this discipline.

We're going to spend more time talking about DSML, automation, and augmentation as they apply to embedded analytics solutions in Chapter 9, but suffice it to say that DSML techniques are often at the center of the prescriptive analytics features we've discussed.

Operationalization (or "Write-Back") of Data

In many cases, the workflows that we've described so far may include steps where data needs to be written back into the data source or other operational system to drive further processes. Here are three real-world examples:

- A user-tracking dashboard shows that a given user has opened a marketing email. The user's record within the CRM system therefore needs to be updated to show that the user has responded to the marketing campaign, which removes them from the recipient list for a period.

- An executive adds a comment about an outlying data point in a chart, which needs to be displayed as a tool tip against that data point for anyone else viewing the chart in the future.

- A user interacts with a dashboard showing errors in a production line. When the user clicks a specific error, a ticket needs to be created in an error-tracking application, containing details about the time and nature of the error.

At a high level, all these examples work in a similar way. Data derived from the embedded *analytics solution* (by the input of the user or derived purely from the data itself) is written back to the *target system* (either a data store within a CRM/ERP system or a dedicated database). In both cases, this achieves the goal of "closing the loop" with an analytics workflow: you use analytics to derive insight and update the data accordingly in a single workflow.

These examples all require some level of integration between the analytics solution and the target system(s), but the key point is that operationalization of data can often be driven from within the embedded analytics solution itself, ensuring that the user can *execute* an actionable insight without leaving the solution.

Operationalization of data as part of an analytics workflow is a highly innovative and heavily invested area for both analytics and data warehousing vendors. For those familiar with OLAP versus online transaction processing (OLTP), the technical distinction between transactional use cases and analytical use cases has historically necessitated different technical approaches and, therefore, different products.

 OLTP use cases usually indicate small volumes of data *written* into a database very frequently, whereas OLAP use cases usually indicate large volumes of data *read* from a database less frequently.

With the advent of scalable SaaS offerings and advances in data storage, caching, and query performance, this distinction is becoming less prevalent. As of the time of writing, some data platform vendors (Snowflake, for example) are working on unified services to provide databases that can address OLAP and OLTP workflows simultaneously: a single store of data that your ERP system writes to *and* that acts as the source of truth your analytics application reads from.

Business Case Integrations

Integrations between messaging applications (like Slack or Microsoft Teams) and data visualization tools are becoming more common. The objective is to ensure that users can access actionable insights even if they're *not* currently using an embedded analytics solution. Here's an example:

1. Vaughn is walking to work, where he's a supply chain manager at a large retail organization. He receives a notification on his messaging app, telling him that inventory levels for a key product line are below a certain warning threshold—a level that Vaughn himself has configured by setting an alert on an embedded analytics object.

2. Clicking the link in the notification, he's directed to the relevant embedded data visualization, which shows him that an expected supplier shipment has been delayed and provides a link to the contact details for the relevant account manager.

3. He clicks the link on his phone, calls the account manager, and confirms that although the shipment is late it will arrive in time to support the expected fulfillment volume for the month, which is also shown in the ERP system alongside the embedded dashboard. It takes Vaughn five minutes to do this, and all before he gets to his office. He decides to stop to buy a coffee to celebrate.

This example has four integration components:

- A methodology for configuring data-driven alerts within the data visualization platform

- A messaging app integration that is targeted by the data visualization platform (along with email and other notification channels)

- A carefully designed dashboard, embedded within the supply chain ERP system

- Appropriate authentication and authorization for Vaughn to interact with these components on his mobile phone

Management and Governance Integrations

Vaughn represents a *consumer* use case, but there are many other powerful integration patterns possible with modern data visualization platforms. Many data visualization and SaaS database tools have RESTful or GraphQL APIs that can be interacted with to perform various key tasks related to management, governance, and reporting.

Lineage and impact analysis can be facilitated by querying the underlying components (KPIs, visualizations, data sources, users, events, etc.) in a data visualization platform to determine the relationships between them. Understanding that a given database holds a table that provides data for a KPI makes it possible to determine the impact that making a change to that component will have. Will it affect one KPI or thousands? This information is very useful for teams managing the development of an embedded analytics solution.

In Figure 5-15, we can see that 29 fields in a data source are derived from 3 tables in a single database. If you're a database administrator about to make a change to one of those tables, it's certainly useful to know that you're potentially going to affect 29 fields used in a Tableau data source.

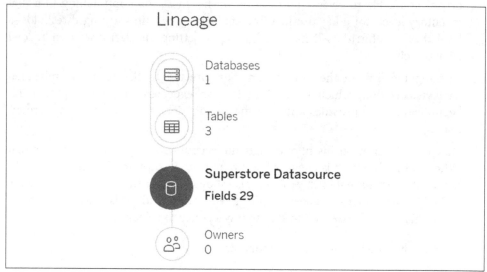

Figure 5-15. An example of how lineage is depicted in Tableau

Here are some other real-world examples where integration with a data visualization platform (usually facilitated by APIs) can solve common governance and management challenges:

Performance auditing
> We've made the case that performance is important, not just in terms of interaction response times, but also overall loading times for embedded objects. Most data visualization platforms include native content or extensible methods to understand basic performance metrics. How fast are my embedded objects loading? Which objects are interacted with the most? What data sources are most popular? All this information is crucial to understand user behavior and support performance tuning initiatives.

Programmatic content management

Programmatic content management can be very useful to deploy, migrate, and update content in an embedded analytics solution. For example, if your solution contains hundreds of embedded objects and you identify that they all contain a calculation that needs to be corrected, having a method to programmatically update the calculation (and potentially redeploy/update/publish the corrected objects) will save a significant amount of time and effort compared to the process of downloading and correcting each object individually.

APIs can be used to address content in this way in many data visualization tools, allowing content, data sources, users, permissions, and group membership all to be managed programmatically. The scope of what you can and can't change is determined by the features provided by the API, so if you're evaluating specific tools, it's always worth looking at any related API references to understand what could potentially be automated.

Programmatic control of user provisioning

Being able to programmatically control user provisioning is of particular relevance to external-facing data monetization products. If you consider a new customer purchasing access to an embedded analytics product, several things may need to happen:

- Payment details may need to be captured and processed.
- The user's details need to be captured and associated with a level of access to the product, depending on options selected at the point of purchase.
- The user needs to be set up in an identity provider or authentication system, as well as within the target systems and the data visualization platform.
- Access permissions need to be applied to control the content the user needs to access. This may extend to objects within the data visualization platform as well as databases, and to the target system as well as non-analytics content hosted on the target system (files, etc.).
- Introductory content (emails, FAQs, login links, etc.) needs to be provided to the user.

Your solution may not require all these processes, and indeed it may not be possible to programmatically address some of them, depending on the nature of the tools used and the features of the available APIs. However, if you're planning the deployment of an embedded analytics solution, it's useful to determine which, if any, of these steps can be automated. Doing so will provide long-term benefits as more users are added.

Conclusion

We've now spent some time exploring the components of an embedded analytics solution and talking about the considerations and the possibilities these solutions can offer. Hopefully, you now have a better understanding of how to approach the planning, development, and implementation of your solution.

In the next chapter, we'll go into more detail about the administration of embedded analytics: setting up users, understanding licensing models, resourcing management, and ownership.

CHAPTER 6

Administration of Embedded Analytics

This chapter will explore the challenges of administering analytics solutions embedded in operational applications. In general, there is one golden rule that governs this process:

> As far as possible, align all the administration of your embedded solution with the administration of the host application.

This ensures minimal duplication of work and better system coordination. We'll also delve into specific topics such as cloud versus on-premises deployment, security configuration, and DevOps integration for a comprehensive understanding of how best to handle these integrated systems.

Deploying Embedded Analytics

When it comes to deciding whether to run embedded analytics on premises or in the cloud, the issues involved can seem quite complex. Businesses of all sizes are moving to cloud storage, as it's generally seen as the best solution for ease of deployment and cost-effectiveness—but there are some edge cases where it's not ideal.

On-Premises Deployment

On premises means your company's server is hosted within your organization's infrastructure and, in many cases, is physically onsite. The server is procured, controlled, administered, maintained, etc., by your company and its in-house IT team or an IT partner. Computers share data and other information through your local network.

Having an on-premises approach can give you the advantage of having control over your architecture, procurement, and scalability. However, there are some drawbacks to this option: it takes longer for hardware to be procured and delivered, and upgrading equipment can be more expensive and difficult. Additionally, scaling is not as straightforward compared with cloud hosting, where availability is not limited by predetermined sizes.

Cloud Deployment

Cloud deployment involves having an external service provider, like Microsoft, Google, or Amazon, manage your data and applications. The service provider takes care of any hardware, software, and other infrastructure needed in its datacenter. Access to these services is often from a browser interface, meaning you can control your account and services from almost anywhere on any device.

Hosting in the cloud makes scaling easier because it allows for greater flexibility and scalability than traditional on-premises hosting. Cloud computing offers an elastic infrastructure that can quickly scale up or down depending on demand, allowing organizations to respond more rapidly to changes in their business environment.

With a cloud provider there is no need for costly hardware investments because resources are available when they're needed and don't require up-front capital investment or the long lead times associated with procuring and configuring physical servers. Instead, all you need to do is request a virtual machine (VM) or Docker container. Typically within minutes, the cloud provider works to match your requirements, allocating additional server resources such as CPU cores, RAM, and disk space to accommodate the requested VM or container size. The process may even involve configuring networking rules for accessibility via an external IP address or private network segment. After these steps have been completed successfully, the newly created instance is ready for use by customers. This simplicity is very attractive!

Although cloud computing offers low costs and simplicity, it can become expensive if not managed carefully. Subscription prices may seem reasonable initially, but increased usage can quickly drive up monthly bills. Additionally, self-service queries created by users are often unoptimized, which could result in a great deal of unnecessary data being read and returned at the expense of compute costs.

In Figure 6-1 you can see a typical application deployment, including single sign-on security, which we will discuss later in this chapter.

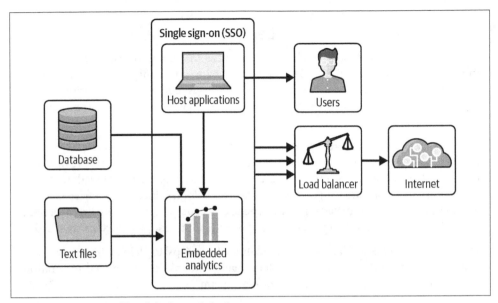

Figure 6-1. A typical load-balanced deployment

It's worth noting the use of a load balancer, such as a load balancing router, to optimize traffic to the internet. A *load balancing router* is a network device used to manage traffic across multiple networks or servers by distributing it among multiple paths to improve performance, reliability, and scalability. Load balancing routers can also be used to balance loads among multiple internet connections or multiple applications running on the same server. Load balancing can be beneficial for embedded analytics, as the load can vary significantly between different clients depending on the user's activity, which could range from simply viewing an embedded report to working with a complex dashboard and visuals to creating self-service objects.

Another approach to deployment, which may be easier to manage, is to use *containers*, discussed later in this chapter.

IT Operations and DevOps for Embedded Analytics

Today most modernized software teams use a DevOps methodology, combining techniques and tools from software development and information technology operations. The aim is to enable more frequent—often continuous—deployments of new features.

DevOps

DevOps is a set of software development practices that combines software development (Dev) and IT operations (Ops). It is designed to enable organizations to deliver applications and services quickly and reliably. DevOps focuses on automation, monitoring, and collaboration to reduce development lifecycles and error-prone manual processes.

There are some disadvantages to this approach, however. Setting up a DevOps environment can be expensive, especially if it requires new investments in software and training. The latter is essential because DevOps requires quite detailed technical knowledge across a wide range of topics and technologies, including source control, automation, observability, testing, infrastructure as code, scripting, and virtualization. With all this, as you can imagine, it can also be difficult to adopt a DevOps standard.

However, for embedded analytics, the ability of DevOps to deliver important new features quickly and with more consistent quality—thanks to automated integration and functional testing—is compelling for many teams.

As DevOps becomes increasingly mainstream, it is naturally important that your embedded analytics solution should support its methodologies. Otherwise, coordinating releases of host applications and embedded analytics may become more complex than necessary and may slow adoption of your solution. In fact, it is common for embedded analytics solutions to get "left behind" by host applications, which are updated more frequently and deployed more easily. On the other hand, in early development, you may wish to iterate numerous deployments of your embedded analytics—adding new charts, for example—without disturbing the deployment of the host application.

Here are some best practices to consider when working with embedded analytics and DevOps:

The embedded analytics solution should integrate with your existing security model.
In general, your embedded analytics security will use the same techniques your DevOps team is currently using for the host application. This way, you won't have to re-create or replicate security information. Security must be integrated into the entire DevOps process, from development to deployment, ensuring that development and testing environments are properly secured, that code is checked for vulnerabilities, that access to production environments is tightly controlled, and that systems are monitored and patched regularly. Additionally, security teams need to be involved in the DevOps process to ensure that the right security measures are put in place and that security goals are met throughout the entire lifecycle of the application.

The DevOps process must support common data scenarios.
Applications incorporating analytics should be able to use data in your existing systems and deliver strong performance across disparate sources, while development is supported by a DevOps methodology. In fact, DevOps, with its extensive automation and ability to spin up multiple environments from scripts, is well suited to developing and testing varied deployments.

No matter what the environment, with prepackaged analytics you can ensure that queries are efficient and well defined. However, for self-service applications that enable end users to do their own data discovery, the queries are not defined by the developers. DevOps should be aware of this and test with inefficient and costly queries of the kind that often arise in self-service scenarios, just as a DBA would do if enabling self-service against a production database.

DevOps should enable you to test against cloud, container, and
hybrid deployment environments.
Embedded analytics should not make life harder or close off options for the DevOps team, now or in the future. The analytics environment needs to work on multiple platforms and in hybrid environments. The DevOps team will look for support for container technologies like Docker and orchestration technologies like Kubernetes for automating deployment, scaling, and management of containerized applications. This ensures that the transition from development, testing, and staging into production, on either physical or virtual machines, runs smoothly. See the sidebar "Containers and the Alternatives" on page 74.

DevOps should be able to deploy using current techniques.
The DevOps teams will not want to work with an embedded analytics platform that forces them to change their current deployment methodology. The platform must be flexible, not only in architecture but in deployment, licensing, and support for high availability. For example, if the host application supports load balancing and failover (perhaps including redundant servers and shared storage devices), then the embedded analytics platform should do so too.

Embedded analytics should support horizontal and vertical scaling.
Horizontal scaling is the process of adding more nodes to a system to increase its capacity. *Vertical scaling* is the process of upgrading individual components within an application architecture without changing any other part of it. An example of vertical scaling is upgrading the RAM on a server; horizontal scaling might involve adding more servers to handle additional load.

Embedded analytics should support continuous integration and delivery.
Many DevOps teams have adopted a continuous integration and continuous delivery (CI/CD) process where code changes are automatically tested and released as they are committed to the code repository.

For this to be efficient, the application logic and user interface of the analytics platform must be decoupled from its data storage layer. This allows developers to work on different parts of an application independently, without worrying about how changes in one part will affect other components. For example, the user interface may see more development and incremental changes than the underlying data storage layer.

Containers and the Alternatives

Traditionally all software ran on physical servers, but in the late 1990s virtual machines emerged as an alternative to running multiple physical computers. VMs enabled IT teams to reduce their costs by consolidating hardware and software resources into a single physical machine, while also providing some flexibility by allowing different operating systems to be run on the same hardware. However, VMs can be slow to start up due to having to boot their entire OS each time they're launched.

More recently, software *containers* have become popular as a lighter-weight alternative to VMs. Containers are a form of operating system virtualization that allows developers to package applications, their dependencies, and libraries into a single unit, called a container. Containers are isolated from the host environment and provide uniformity, portability, and scalability across different operating systems. Containers launch much faster and with less memory consumption than VMs and can be easily deployed across different infrastructures.

Docker is a popular container platform that creates and manages containers. It uses images, which are preconfigured packages of software that can be used to quickly deploy applications. It also has built-in orchestration tools for managing multiple containers.

Kubernetes is an open source container orchestration platform that automates the deployment, scaling, and management of containerized applications. It is used to run, manage, and scale distributed applications, and works with Docker, Google Cloud Platform (GCP), and other container technologies. Kubernetes simplifies the process of deploying and managing containerized workloads.

Virtual machines still have some advantages. For example, they provide better isolation between different environments, as each VM has its own OS and application stack that can't be accessed by other machines or applications running on the same physical hardware—something that's not possible with containers due their shared nature. Also, if you need to access legacy systems, then using VMs may still be the best option, since there often isn't support available for containerized versions of these types of software.

Security for Embedded Analytics

When designing an embedded solution, security must be the first priority. Data is at the core of analytics and should always be protected accordingly: there could be legal and monetary implications to not protecting it. To ensure successful administration, it is recommended that you use existing security infrastructure and controls provided by the host application rather than create new ones specifically for analytics. This simplifies management, while also preventing potential gaps in safety that could lead to a breach in security.

Security Priorities for an Embedded Analytics Solution

Successful embedded analytics solutions will prioritize these security considerations:

Adaptable options

It is important to ensure that your enterprise's security solutions are equipped with the necessary features for multiple scenarios, such as operational reports and self-service analytics. Although initially you may only need embedded analytics capabilities, having options available in case of future success will be beneficial. For those selling shrink-wrapped applications featuring analytical functions, investing now in long-term flexibility will prove advantageous down the line.

Permissions

Administrators should have the ability to set controls and permissions either for individual users or by roles, depending on the scenario. For example, role-based security is essential when embedded analytics are being accessed by multiple users in operational applications; however, if more personalization is desired (e.g., for management or executive dashboards), it may be necessary to assign specific user permissions that do not match traditional organizational roles, such as giving a head of sales access to reports from marketing that other members of sales cannot view.

Multitenant support

When implementing an embedded analytics solution in a multitenant host application, it is essential to consider how security as well as user and resource management are handled for each tenant. Not only should control of users and resources between tenants be managed securely, but additional resources, such as templates for dashboard or report design, integrated documentation, and customization options, need to be managed as well. It is important that these secondary resources are stored safely; if they are not secured within the database by the tenant host, then appropriate measures must be taken to ensure they cannot cross over into another tenant's environment. Even though this may seem unimportant in single-tenancy environments, when working with multiple tenants, all data needs to be treated as confidential company information, regardless of its perceived importance.

Integration with third-party standards

A solution that can provide robust support should adhere to standards like LDAP and integrate with directory services, such as Microsoft Active Directory. This integration allows user authentication data and other security information, including passwords, to be securely shared across the network between various devices or applications in an enterprise system. Furthermore, role-based access control can easily be implemented, since roles are already defined within Active Directory.

Standalone security model

In some cases, you may need to create and implement a standalone security model. In these situations, the embedded technology must have a suitable internal security system to meet your standards and a comprehensive, well-documented API.

With these priorities in mind, let's look at some different approaches to security that may be useful.

Open and Closed Systems

A truly *open system* allows all users access to view and modify any shared content. This could be convenient for small teams or companies that have an open policy with data in general. However, due to the potential dangers associated with such unrestricted sharing, we cannot recommend this approach.

For medium-sized teams and companies, a *restricted open system* is recommended. This type of system restricts access to shared content in some way, making it permissible for certain users to edit particular pieces of content, while others may not be able to view the same information at all. Additionally, if you want your content accessible for viewing by everyone, but only editable by a select few, then this type of open system with restrictions would work.

Most large enterprises and nearly all multitenant platforms use some variation of a *closed system*. In a closed system, administrators can only view and manage user accounts where they share the same user security group. This restriction also applies to groups of which they are members; admins cannot access any other users or groups outside their own. Consequently, there is no longer an *all users* group on such systems, meaning it's impossible for all users in the system to be referred to as one collective entity.

If you are providing services to multiple tenants or companies, it is essential that you establish distinct groups for each one. We highly advise using a closed system in cases where customers have clients from different businesses and organizations who should remain unaware of the existence of other users on the platform.

Having decided on your security approach, there are several ways in which you can configure how a user signs on to the operational application and the embedded analytics. The most common and recommended method is single sign-on.

Single Sign-on

SSO is an authentication process that allows a user to access multiple applications or websites with one set of login credentials. SSO reduces the need for users to remember and manage different usernames and passwords, making it easier for them to log in to their accounts from any device without having to manually enter their details each time they want access.

When deploying embedded analytics, SSO support is essential to enable a seamless experience for users, with no special login required for the analytic features. Instead, users will be authenticated through your host application.

SSO embedding works by adding a login button to an application (or adding a function to an existing login button) that enables users to log in using their SSO credentials. When the user clicks on this button, they are redirected to the designated *identity provider* (IdP) page, where they can enter their username and password once before being granted access to both the host and embedded systems without having to manually input additional details for each one.

For a secure, standards-based way to exchange authentication and authorization data between an IdP and a *service provider* (SP), most developers use Security Assertion Markup Language (SAML). The embedded analytics system will usually act as the service provider, and the operational system that verifies the user's identity will be the IdP.

This process of consolidating identities and authentication methods is called *federation*. There are two common ways to use federation for embedded analytics:

Service provider–initiated flow
> In an SP-initiated flow, when a user attempts to access protected resources they are redirected to the identity provider's login page. This method allows users who already have accounts in both systems to quickly log in to applications without having multiple sets of usernames and passwords.

> In embedded analytics, where the analytic system is the service provider and the host application the identity provider, this scenario is most useful when the business has some standalone analytics applications but also uses the same vendor's features for embedding.

Identity provider–initiated flow

In an IdP-initiated flow—the preferred option for embedded analytics—when a user attempts to access protected resources from the host application they are redirected to the service provider's login page, where they can enter credentials and authenticate with SAML.

Even better for the user, an identity provider can use an API to log in to the service provider on their behalf, with all the necessary information (including signed security tokens) needed for them to authenticate via SAML on the SP side. This results in higher user adoption and satisfaction because it feels more natural to the user and enables the embedded analytics to feel like a complete component of the overall system.

In general, look for a system that works with identity providers that support SAML 2.0, such as Okta, Auth0, or Active Directory Federation Services (AD FS). Some enterprise applications, such as Salesforce, have their own identity providers that enable your users to use their logins for those applications to interact with your embedded systems.

Summary of Security Practices

Security should always be taken seriously to ensure both the safety of your customers' information and regulatory compliance. Here are some key points to keep in mind:

- If you provide analytics to customers or partners as a service or product, you should use a separate instance of the analytics server for this. This ensures that your own systems are isolated from external users.

- Take the same approach for data. The data connected to your analytics server should not include any data that external users must not access.

- Enable a *closed system*.

- Choose an embedded architecture that supports SAML 2.0 and use strong authentication for your embedded instances, such as Auth0, Okta, or AD FS.

- Use the IdP-initiated scenario for SSO with an API for authentication.

- Ensure that logging of security events is enabled: who logs in, who accesses which data, and so forth.

Other Administrative Considerations

Deployment and security will be your primary administrative concerns, but there are some other administrative features to consider, such as scheduling, version management, report bursting, and the admin console.

Scheduling

It is rarely efficient or, if running in the cloud, cost-effective to update an operational report or dashboard every time a user accesses it. This is especially true if the object is embedded in a screen that is always open on the user's desktop. You will need the ability to refresh reports on a schedule or in response to event triggers from the host application. Integration with an existing enterprise scheduler, or a scheduler built into the database platform, may be useful if the enterprise already uses scheduled jobs extensively.

Version Management

If you are using DevOps processes, you will most likely integrate your embedded analytics with your existing version control system. Otherwise, you should ensure the embedded technology includes a built-in version management system. This may be critical for organizations with specific compliance standards that demand strict versioning of generated reports, such as in health care and financial services, where administrators need to guarantee accuracy of records over time so any changes are tracked, monitored, and can be easily reverted if necessary.

Report Bursting

Report bursting, as shown in Figure 6-2, is a process of distributing preformatted reports to different recipients. It usually involves splitting the report into multiple parts, each containing specific data related to that recipient's needs and interests.

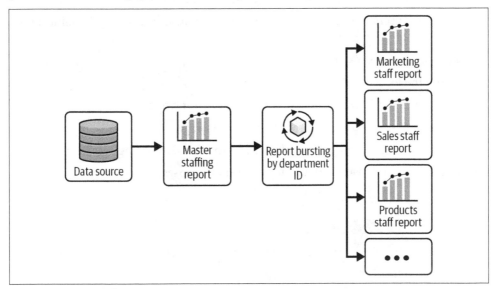

Figure 6-2. Report bursting

Report bursting allows admins to customize individual versions based on criteria such as company name, department, and so on, meaning that each recipient receives the correct version of the report that contains their own specific information.

Bursting is often used for invoice generation, financial reporting (creating a master report that is burst into individual cost center reports for managers), or even pay slips for employees.

The Administrative Console

A good analytics solution should provide a centralized user interface for administrators to manage server resources, clustering, schedulers, security configurations, and all other tasks they are responsible for. This unified portal or console offers admins an efficient way to view the allocation and utilization of their resources. This is not only more convenient, but also increasingly necessary to ensure proper governance of the company's systems and understand how assets are being utilized.

Common tasks that can be completed from a console may include the following:

- Configuring the embedded analytics web server, including connection information and security certificate
- Configuring logging, whether built in or using a logging service
- Configuring international and localized settings such as language, currency, date formats, and perhaps character encoding
- Integrating with Active Directory or another directory service
- Managing users and user groups, including creating accounts, changing privileges, and group membership
- Scheduling refreshes of data
- Setting the location of temporary storage
- Configuring or deleting artifacts created by self-service users
- Monitoring server performance and resource usage
- Canceling long-running or "stuck" queries that are consuming resources
- Backing up (and restoring) data for recovery purposes

Conclusion

The administration of embedded analytics in any context always involves a combination of (or a compromise between) the management of the host application and the requirements of the analytics platform. For this reason, it is important to choose platforms that are not merely compatible, but well aligned in their approach to administration, security, and governance in general.

In the next chapter we'll look at data governance in more detail, as it has become a significant consideration, if not a headache, for data administrators and developers. We will see that embedded analytics share many of the governance concerns of standalone applications, with a few unique requirements of their own.

CHAPTER 7

Governance and Compliance

Almost every day we read of data breaches, the egregious misuse of customer information, or some new hacking scandal. In this treacherous environment, any company using data extensively must grapple with ever more regulation and acute consumer pressure. As a result, the security and privacy of their data is top of mind for both anxious executives and hard-pressed IT teams.

Data governance as a practice has grown over the years from relatively simple policies for security and privacy to a broad, enterprise-wide initiative covering not only access to data, but the uses of data in analytics and machine learning and even the purposes of data for marketing, sales, research, and so on.

In Chapter 6 we considered some of the particular security questions that embedded analytics raise. These questions are potent because we are combining two particular kinds of data: operational data in the host application and analytic data that has been integrated, cleansed, and often denormalized to enable efficient analysis. Just as analytics can be a valuable source of insight for business, it can also be a gold mine for less welcome use cases if it's not rigorously protected.

In this chapter we'll look beyond the security issues to include the demands of privacy, governance, and compliance. Let's start with some definitions.

Governance, Compliance, Security, and Privacy

It can be useful to visualize the components of data oversight as a Venn diagram of overlapping interests, as in Figure 7-1.

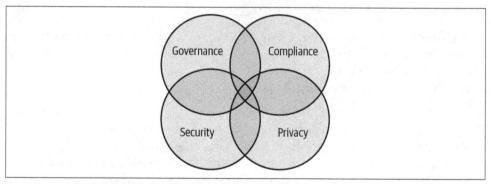

Figure 7-1. The fields of data oversight and assurance

These four areas are closely related—all are concerned with some aspect of the safety and assurance of our data and the oversight of our processes—but we need to be clear that they are also quite different. These differences require us to take a variety of approaches to ensure we are covering all the possibilities of risk.

To be free from threat and to be free from unwanted attention or intrusion are basic human needs that, nevertheless, vary widely in their terms between different societies and social contexts. Even when discussing data security and privacy in the context of regulations there are important, but subtle, differences between different regulatory regimes. So, the specific definitions that apply in your circumstances will vary, but it is still useful to have some principles in mind to guide your thinking.

Privacy and Security

Privacy is about appropriate use of personal data.

Security is about protecting data from unauthorized access.

If we take *privacy* to mean that freedom from unwanted attention or intrusion mentioned earlier, and *security* the need to be free from threat, then a simple analogy may make the important differences clear.

In your home, if your blinds are open and anyone can look in, you have little privacy, even though with the doors and windows locked, you feel secure. However, if your blinds are closed but the door is unlocked, despite your sense of privacy, which no passerby can casually breach, you are not secure: if someone enters through your unlocked door, your privacy as well as your security have been compromised.

In terms of data, think of the controls you have in place to ensure the security of your network, such as firewalls and logins. You may be secure from unauthorized access, but if you have not taken care to ensure that even authenticated users do not casually see what they are not meant to see, you are not protecting privacy.

On the other hand, perhaps you have put in place protections to ensure that only users with the right permissions see certain data. You have done your best to protect privacy in that context. Yet, if the network is vulnerable, unauthorized users may still insinuate themselves, and if they acquire the right privileges, both security and privacy are breached.

It is very important to understand, in any given scenario, what you are protecting: is it security or privacy? The answer is often both, but you will still find it best to consider them as separate issues and address them with specific solutions.

Governance and Compliance

Governance is the management framework used to ensure processes support an organization's goals and objectives.

Compliance focuses on meeting legal and regulatory requirements.

If your governance program is motivated in the first place by the need to keep on the right side of regulation, then compliance will likely be your first concern. Understand, however, that while governance and compliance are closely related, we must make some important distinctions.

Governance is the process of ensuring that you have sound processes in place and that these processes are diligently followed:

Governance is not about making better decisions.

Governance is about making decisions the right way.

This is quite a paradox for some, but we think it is realistic. We have been focusing on decision support and how to make better decisions. A good process should enable better decisions but cannot guarantee it.

If you think about civic governance, for example local government, you can see the difference quite clearly. You may not agree with the decisions your local government makes, such as approving a new building or building a new traffic island, but that is quite different from believing that it has arrived at those decisions through a corrupt or invalid process.

Compliance depends on meeting a predefined set of criteria. These requirements may be external (laws, contracts, etc.) or internal (such as codes of practice). You can think of compliance as a checklist: do you meet this set of requirements, whether issued by a government, a professional body, or your own code of practice? You will either be compliant or not.

It is difficult to consistently comply with regulations if you are not well governed. Without a thorough policy, broken processes are more likely to lurk somewhere in your organization or architecture. Still, even a well-governed organization may not be fully compliant because it may have overlooked or misunderstood some aspect of the rules or not kept up with changes to them. When this happens, your internal processes, however carefully administered, miss the target.

Policies and Practices

A full review of data governance best practices is a specialized topic, beyond the scope of this book. But we can provide some simple guidelines—some rules of thumb—that are relevant to the kinds of governance and compliance issues that crop up when embedding analytics.

From Gatekeepers to Shopkeepers

When describing new patterns of ownership for data and analytics, it's helpful to describe IT's role—and IT's mindset—as moving from being gatekeepers to shopkeepers.

The defensive approach no longer works so well in modern business intelligence strategy because it nearly always includes a strong element of self-service. Increasingly, users have the skills and tools to do their own analysis, but still they need data.

Traditionally, IT teams saw themselves as gatekeepers of the enterprise system, effectively keeping unwanted intruders out of important data sources. However, this model is typically too restrictive for all but the most regulated of new scenarios. Indeed, there is a real danger that the process is so constrained that even well-intentioned business users will work around the system rather than within it, creating

---

so-called shadow systems. These unsanctioned pools of data may be a considerable threat to governance in themselves.

It can be better for IT team members to think of their roles less as gatekeepers and more like shopkeepers. The shopkeeper is not unregulated (think of tobacco, alcohol, or lottery sales) but does ensure that products (or in our case, data) are fit for purpose, appropriately packaged, and available when needed. The advantage of this approach is that well-provisioned users (customers in the data shop) get what they need in a well-governed form, without the danger of being overprivileged with access to significant data sources. In short, rather than letting users *into* a system to explore, you push the appropriate data—and only the appropriate data—*out* to the user.

If Compliance Is Critical, You Need a Compliance Team

Many of us work in highly regulated sectors such as public service, health care, finance, and so on. It is important, therefore, to remember that governance does not guarantee compliance, but is necessary to achieve consistency and confidence. We strongly suggest, as part of a governance program, that you set up a cross-functional team tasked with keeping on top of compliance issues. It should continuously re-evaluate legislation and identify where you need more, better, or new coverage with your policies as well as look into incidents and issues and track the numbers.

Not taking compliance for granted is a good practice in itself, but it also helps to relieve some burden and anxiety from others. It's a big responsibility for a database administrator, for example, to keep on top of health care data-handling legislation and keep your systems running. Good policies frame the path to compliance; they are not barriers to business.

Consumers and customers worldwide are increasingly worried about data privacy and, with good reason, don't have much trust in enterprises to have their best interests at heart. Here are some steps you can take to improve customers' confidence in your business:

Be straightforward about your privacy policies and give customers control.
    We are all familiar with websites that ask us to specify our cookie policy. You can, and should, ask customers whether they agree to other uses of data you may have about them, such as demographics for research, usage of the system for product improvements, and trends for marketing.

Put policies in place at every level of the enterprise that enforce these preferences as rules.
    Some rules can be applied in code or technical procedures. For example, you can check that you are not extracting demographic data from a customer record into the warehouse unless the customer has given permission. Other rules, such as "don't use these customer records for product research," may be more like policies. Either way, your governance program needs to cover them.

Look for Secondary Benefits of Good Governance

So far, these practices have been focused on what you may think of as the restrictive aspects of governance: trying not to do the wrong thing. Good governance also enables a lot of good to happen.

A well-governed infrastructure improves access to data and encourages efficient reuse of analytics and reports that have already been created. This works because policies define in advance what data is relevant and permissible to a role, and it can therefore be confidently provisioned. Poorly governed systems tend to raise a stream of ad hoc requests for data access, which are disruptive for IT and prone to error, including the compliance risk of overprovisioning permissions just to get the job done.

Although better decisions are not the direct goal of governance, a well-governed decision is likely to be better understood and more widely supported. Confidence in the process lends confidence to the decision, especially if the policies have been crafted as a partnership between teams rather than assembled along departmental lines.

Collaboration can improve in a well-governed organization. Many chief information officers (CIOs) complain about data silos in their business or data hoarding by departments and individuals. These are real problems often caused by data owners being unsure of whether users outside their span of control will handle data responsibly. With the right policies in place, data owners feel more comfortable that there will be accountability when it comes to sharing and collaboration. Sometimes the responsibility for this more open use of data will fall to the chief technical officer (CTO), if there is no one holding the specific CIO title.

Commit to Openness, Awareness, and Training

If data users don't know about a governance program, it cannot be effective. Several of these practices build on a shared understanding of the governance process across your organization:

- Be open about the program, its goals, and its measures of success. Publish the strategy, describe the processes, and share the metrics.
- Make awareness of the program part of onboarding. If you have compliance training for other areas, such as harassment prevention, work with those teams and HR to get data governance onto a similar track.
- Include relevant elements of the governance strategy (and how it is specifically realized in the tools and platforms under review) in all technical training related to data, such as training on BI tools.
- Cover the importance of data quality in training sessions and how policies help maintain that quality, along with the availability and reuse of governed data

sources. Data analysts and report authors in particular should not feel they are trading agility for policy. Rather, they should see governed data as a resource opening up possibilities for more assertive work.

- Help users by addressing their use cases with documentation and FAQs. If a user needs to download some data (exporting it to a file, perhaps), where can it be stored? When can it be deleted? How can a user request a specific data feed or extract from IT if they can't self-serve?

- Implement a "governance assured" stamp of approval, which you can add to dashboards, reports, and other artifacts to show that the data in question has been governed properly.

Governing Your Governance

An effective governance program is a continuous effort and will be unique to your organization: no single approach is right for everyone. As an organization, you will adopt new technologies and platforms. In addition, new roles will emerge and regulations will change. When these things happen, you'll need to work out how your specific program can be extended to govern them.

It should be clear, then, that you need to regularly evaluate your policies. How often? Certainly an annual assessment makes sense at a minimum, because over that period a lot can change. Other reviews will be ad hoc, for example when completing a merger or acquisition that brings new data, new people, and new tools on board.

Some sectors, such as financial services, may see frequent changes as not only legislation about data but also rules concerning money laundering, sanctions, liquidity, credit, and so on, evolve over time. Keeping track of this changing legislative landscape can be an arduous exercise.

One concern that may be more relevant in a large organization, or one with very strict governance needs, is where governance should sit in the management hierarchy. Does the governance team report to the CTO or CIO? Or perhaps to a chief security officer or a chief compliance officer? Different organizations adopt different configurations. How well they work can depend on the specific fit of individuals to roles, as well as on whether there is a strong commitment throughout the organization to making the program successful.

We hold the view that security is related to governance but is a separate, specialized domain. Compliance is also related to governance, so a chief security officer or a chief compliance officer may well manage a governance team, directly or indirectly.

If neither of these roles exist, having the governance team report to the CIO rather than the CTO is preferable. It might even be better for them to report to the CFO; this happens in effect in many organizations where the CIO reports to the CFO.

We often find we need to emphasize that governance is not a technology problem with a technical solution. Rather, it emerges as an issue of people, processes, and technologies working together, and the office of the CIO may be the best fit to oversee it. No ideal configuration exists: what matters is that the organization's structure should support, rather than constrain, your strategy and objectives.

A Security and Privacy Cross-Functional Team

With an understanding that security and privacy are separate but associated domains, you'll find it practical to establish two separate but associated programs, even if these programs are run by one team.

The focus of a privacy program should be on the relevant legislation that determines your data processing, protection, and retention requirements. The program must also take into account consumer expectations. Realistically, compliance with regulations will be at the top of the agenda. If regulations in your field are complex, such as in health care, you may need a legal specialist on the privacy team, perhaps from your office of general counsel.

The requirements identified by the privacy program are passed to the security program for implementation. However, they shouldn't specify the specific processes or technologies to be implemented.

It's the security team that has the knowledge and capability to set up suitable protections and controls to meet the needs identified by the privacy program. An important advantage of keeping the two separated in this way is that the interpretation of regulations won't be unduly influenced by concerns about technical limitations. As a result, when the security team reviews the unbiased requirements from the privacy program, it's possible they'll identify technical demands that require new, or different, tools and platforms.

Governance in the Cloud

As we saw in Chapter 6, it's a sound practice to define and implement security and privacy controls at the lowest practical tier—as close to your data storage as possible. Benefits will bubble up from there. In the cloud, however, there's another consideration. You should look to the underlying cloud platform itself to provide excellent security and privacy features. The more support the platform provides, the less you have to worry about and the more consistently you can apply your best practices.

With this support from the platform, an enterprise deploying analytics in the cloud will find security less daunting. Encryption, for example, is a critical feature for both security and privacy. Look for comprehensive encryption features in your data storage platform. You should not have to design and implement such demanding features yourself when your cloud provider has greater expertise and resources to make them available as part of your subscription. Securing the entire cloud infrastructure is not a role for the analytics administrator or developer, although it is useful to know the basics.

Business Continuity Is a Security and Privacy Issue

It's one thing to protect your data when your systems are running smoothly, but you also have to consider its resiliency and availability in the event of an adverse incident. For customers and users, it's infuriating enough when a system is down. They want service restored quickly, and not just because they want to get back to work. In the darkness of downtime, they can't help but worry that their interests have been compromised: the wait is too often a protracted agony, relieved only when the application is back up and running. Think of how you feel when you can't access your bank accounts online: it's not just an inconvenience, but a real worry.

Some consumer-focused legislation, such as the European Union's GDPR (*https:// oreil.ly/MA5Oj*), explicitly refers to this critical need by requiring that the organization "implement appropriate technical and organisational measures" that include "the ability to restore the availability and access to personal data in a timely manner in the event of a physical or technical incident."

Cloud services are typically very robust and reliable, but outages do happen. It is critical to ensure your cloud service not only automatically performs regular database backups, but also guarantees *point-in-time restore* from these backups.

Developing a Governance Strategy

Some companies worry that governance will be disruptive to their work, or a burden that holds them back, or an extra expense that they must budget for. But the truth is that you are already doing some data governance right now, and you can develop a strategy starting from where you are. In fact, it is best to do just that.

Today, you may not have a documented data governance policy, but you certainly have people who manage your data: a database administrator who sets permissions for access, IT staff who diligently back up and restore files, a network manager who checks that your BI tools are licensed properly. And you will likely have some form of data quality controls or processes in place.

To start where you are, create a directory of the data assets that your organization works with. At the same time, add a listing of who exercises responsibilities for that data—whether they are an administrator, a manager, or just an engineer plowing a lonely furrow—and find out who they report to.

In the course of this investigation, you will likely find some sobering, if not shocking, oversights and gaps in coverage that need quick attention. There may be software developers, finance business controllers, and other employees who have stored data on a machine underneath their desk or in some private database, or even in the cloud. At the end, you will have a catalog of assets, roles, and accountabilities. It's going to be informal, and perhaps a little messy, but it will reflect your present-day organization and your needs.

It is too much to ask, and too risky, to remodel your organization to better govern your data. Instead, construct some formal scaffolding around your existing ad hoc structures. You can do that by identifying some of the key roles involved.

Who advises or is consulted on what the governance controls should be? This might include business users, the office of general counsel, and IT teams. It is best at first to cast the net widely; you will soon learn who has useful insights to share.

Who implements the controls? Some aspects of this work can be quite technical, like applying row- and column-level permissions in a database. Others may be more administrative, like HR ensuring that a new hire is assigned the right job title so they inherit the right permissions automatically.

Measuring the Success of Governance

Data governance strategies may not seem to have a measurable impact on a business's bottom line, but if things go wrong, they can. Regulators may impose heavy fines and require restitution. There is also reputational risk to consider. So we can certainly say that bad governance, or none at all, may indeed have a financial impact.

Still, "not getting fined" is not a great KPI for your annual review. How else might you measure the success of a governance program?

One way is to specifically identify data-related issues and incidents as part of your existing IT issue management system, while also ensuring that all data-related incidents are reviewed for governance implications. For example, a user losing access to a database may be a simple incident, but if it is resolved by elevating their permissions to give them access to more data than they strictly need, that would be a governance issue.

Recording, investigating, and tracking such cases will result in a body of knowledge and associated metrics about how governance is improving or degrading over time.

In addition to incidents, which are by their nature exceptions to the regular running of your systems, it is useful to measure overall system performance. For example, by tracking how many users have access to a system, what their permissions are, and how much they use it, you can establish a useful benchmark and, over time, develop insights into how the data is being used.

At first, you may not have a good sense of whether a metric is improving or not as it changes, but these insights will help. For example, if you are adding more users, it may be because of increased data literacy, which is a good thing. But if those users are creating more copies of the data in more reports without reuse, that would suggest poor governance.

In short, tracking incidents and issues is crucial to your success. Measures of insight and oversight develop over time and can be useful benchmarks once you understand what you are looking for.

Summary

This has been a very brief overview of governance and compliance policy as it may affect embedded analytics. Let's review some of the important ideas.

The move from being gatekeepers, who prevent data access, to shopkeepers, who enable it, is a key element of embedding analytics. The purpose of the work is to bring data and insight to new users and new scenarios.

The distinctions between security, privacy, governance, and compliance are useful to bear in mind when addressing issues, especially across team boundaries. Determining whether something is a governance or compliance issue, and whether it concerns privacy or security, can unlock important and insightful conversations.

Finally, you can begin to develop a data governance strategy even from a seemingly unpromising and informal starting point. The trick is to get started. It is much easier to improve governance gradually than it is to handle the problems that can arise from a poorly governed infrastructure.

We have seen one reason why governance is so important to both consumers and businesses: a growing awareness of governance issues among increasingly data-literate business users. But there is also expanding concern about the security and privacy of data, which is keenly felt when decisions are made not by human beings, but by automated systems.

Automation of decisions has an important role to play in the future of embedded analytics. In Chapter 9, we'll look at some scenarios and techniques where machine intelligence and decision making can be combined with embedded analytics.

Meanwhile, in the next chapter, we'll consider the most used (if not the most popular) analytic tool of all—the spreadsheet.

CHAPTER 8

Beyond the Spreadsheet

Spreadsheets have an uneasy coexistence with visual analytics solutions. Most visual analytics professionals have plentiful stories about how difficult it can be to drive adoption in environments where spreadsheets are considered the default option for working with data. No matter how sophisticated and interactive a visual experience is, the cry from users in the real world is often "Can I get this in Excel?"

However, over the last few years spreadsheet tools have developed at a pace comparable to visual analytics, with new paradigms and features that enable users to use spreadsheet tools as the heart of accessible, collaborative, and programmable *platforms* centered around their data. Some of these tools are driving the development of entirely new analytics approaches, some eschew the entire concept of visual analytics in favor of grids and tables, and some are purely designed to democratize the process of collecting and managing a single source of truth (SSOT) for data within an organization.

So, how should we consider spreadsheets in relation to embedded analytics? In this chapter we'll explore some of the history behind spreadsheets, see how the product landscape has evolved over the last few years, and bring to life ways in which modern spreadsheet tools can add real value to an embedded analytics solution.

To help support conversations about tools you may have within your own organization, we'll also attempt to answer the question of whether spreadsheet tools can be considered as analytics platforms in their own right.

Setting the Stage

For the purposes of this chapter, let's set out some loose definitions to help us differentiate terms that are often used interchangeably in the real world:

Tables

> The typical way in which data is represented and interacted with in a spreadsheet tool. We're using this term to encompass the most basic examples, where data is organized into rows that share common columns, and more complex examples like pivot tables. Synonyms might include terms like "sheets" or "grids."

Raw data

> The source of data used by a spreadsheet tool. This might be as simple as row-level, disaggregated data that's been pasted into a sheet in your spreadsheet tool. It could also be data stored in a relational database that the spreadsheet tool connects to.

Delimited data

> This term encompasses a variety of file formats that are used to encode and exchange data generated by databases, ERP and CRM systems, and spreadsheet tools. Data in a delimited text file is arranged in rows, with a delimiter character used to separate the values in each row into columns. As mentioned in Chapter 4, different characters can be used as delimiters; the most common example is a comma, used in a CSV file.
>
> As much as delimited data is a primary way of exchanging data between systems, whether an analytics solution provides options to export delimited data from a system is a contentious point when trying to promote adoption, governance, and best-practice administration—a point we'll cover later.

Spreadsheet tool

> The software that enables you to create and manipulate raw data and tables. We're going to use this term to encompass ubiquitous software like Excel along with more modern derivatives that leverage similar functionality to provide SaaS-based platforms with broad features, like Airtable and Google Sheets.

Let There Be Spreadsheets

Over the last two hundred thousand years, humans have evolved to be pattern recognition and "visual enumeration" machines. Our peripheral vision and visual acuity are vital traits that enabled early humans to evade predators, hunt, and make critical decisions about the environment around them. Our whole view of the world is informed by these traits.

What does this have to do with embedded analytics and spreadsheets? Clearly, it's a bit of a stretch to compare an ancient human evading predators with someone sitting in an air-conditioned office reviewing their latest marketing reports, but some of the ways we see and interpret data still tap into these ancient behaviors. Let's consider some examples.

Figure 8-1 illustrates a great example of *selection*. It's important (even potentially lifesaving) for us to be able to recognize ripe fruits, so we're able to very quickly identify common visual traits—a change of color, in this case—and group those elements together as a single selection that we're interested in.

Figure 8-1. Ripening apples on a tree

Figure 8-2 shows us how this selection trait can apply to a more modern (but perhaps less tasty) example. Highlighting rows of data according to a condition leverages our ability to quickly identify the rows we're interested in. Notice how it's intuitive to scan through the list of sales reps and identify the names of four individuals. This is your visual selection trait in action.

◢	A	B	C	D	E	F	G
1	OrderDate	Region	Rep	Item	Units	Unit Cost	Total
2	44202	East	Jones	Pencil	95	1.99	189.05
3	44219	Central	Kivell	Binder	50	19.99	999.5
4	44236	Central	Jardine	Pencil	36	4.99	179.64
5	44253	Central	Gill	Pen	27	19.99	539.73
6	44270	West	Sorvino	Pencil	56	2.99	167.44
7	44287	East	Jones	Binder	60	4.99	299.4
8	44304	Central	Andrews	Pencil	75	1.99	149.25
9	44321	Central	Jardine	Pencil	90	4.99	449.1
10	44338	West	Thompson	Pencil	32	1.99	63.68
11	44355	East	Jones	Binder	60	8.99	539.4
12	44372	Central	Morgan	Pencil	90	4.99	449.1
13	44389	East	Howard	Binder	29	1.99	57.71
14	44406	East	Parent	Binder	81	19.99	1619.19
15	44423	East	Jones	Pencil	35	4.99	174.65
16	44440	Central	Smith	Desk	2	125	250

Figure 8-2. Selection as applied to tabular data

Enumeration is another key trait tied to our visual acuity. Figure 8-3 shows a potentially dangerous situation for an ancient human: a clan of hyenas looking particularly curious. How do we evaluate this danger? One hyena is unlikely to present a serious threat, but a group, certainly one as large as this, is something to be worried about. There's a nuance here: we're not counting the individuals in the group; we just instinctively know that a group of this size is dangerous. Fortunately, our modern world rarely involves such danger, but the trait is still useful.

Figure 8-3. A clan of hyenas

Using the same example set of data, Figure 8-4 shows how we can enumerate quantities very quickly, without explicitly counting values. Most readers would be able to instantly determine that there are more pencils than binders in the selected column, just by virtue of some basic highlighting.

	A	B	C	D	E	F	G
1	OrderDate	Region	Rep	Item	Units	Unit Cost	Total
2	44202	East	Jones	Pencil	95	1.99	189.05
3	44219	Central	Kivell	Binder	50	19.99	999.5
4	44236	Central	Jardine	Pencil	36	4.99	179.64
5	44253	Central	Gill	Pencil	27	19.99	539.73
6	44270	West	Sorvino	Pencil	56	2.99	167.44
7	44287	East	Jones	Binder	60	4.99	299.4
8	44304	Central	Andrews	Pencil	75	1.99	149.25
9	44321	Central	Jardine	Pencil	90	4.99	449.1
10	44338	West	Thompson	Pencil	32	1.99	63.68
11	44355	East	Jones	Binder	60	8.99	539.4
12	44372	Central	Morgan	Pencil	90	4.99	449.1
13	44389	East	Howard	Binder	29	1.99	57.71
14	44406	East	Parent	Binder	81	19.99	1619.19
15	44423	East	Jones	Pencil	35	4.99	174.65
16	44440	Central	Smith	Desk	2	125	250

Figure 8-4. Enumerating quantities

We have demonstrated a few traits that are well suited to interpreting data arranged in a table, but there's one particular trait that was arguably the genesis for the *very first* use of written tables in history: pattern recognition. We are pattern recognition machines, able to instinctively find structure and repeating visual motifs in the world around us, outperforming even the most sophisticated algorithms.

Figure 8-5 shows a pattern we're all familiar with: footprints in sand. Subconsciously we may be determining who or what left the prints. Footprints also have *direction*, which gives us even more rich information about the immediate surroundings: we can determine where they come from and where they lead. How does this relate to interpretation of real-world data in our example?

Figure 8-5. Footprints in sand

Figure 8-6 is possibly the very first use of a "table" to represent data for interpretation. It's a multiplication table believed to be around 2,300 years old. The table relies on directional pattern recognition to allow a viewer to select multipliers from a given row and column, then find the intersection between them to determine the product.

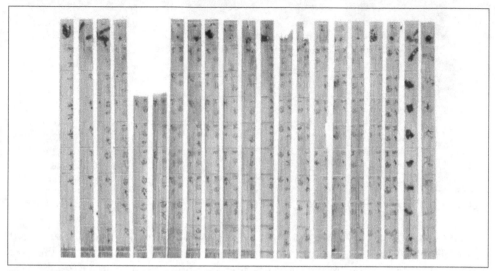

Figure 8-6. A section of the oldest known multiplication table

The full version of this table allows the multiplication of any whole or half integers between 0.5 and 99.5. It's a fascinating example of how tables evolved to solve real-world problems, and a use case that's still found across the world today, on blackboards, in books, and—you guessed it—in Excel.

Are Spreadsheets Analytics Platforms?

Written tables stemming from the multiplication table example in Figure 8-6 were the first way humans were able to systematically and rigorously interpret data, which is a solid definition of "analytics" as we know it today.

However, it took the advent of personal computing in the late 1970s to give us a glimpse of the truly transformative change that spreadsheets could bring about. The first commercially available spreadsheet tool, VisiCalc (Figure 8-7), was made available for the Apple II computer in 1979, and the impact was immediate. Manual bookkeeping processes, laborious calculations, and error-prone repetition were eradicated with recomputable formulas, easily navigable tables, and consistent data entry methods. Finance teams adopted the technology, their companies saved millions of dollars, and the concept of the modern spreadsheet was born.

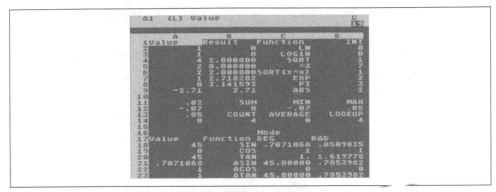

Figure 8-7. VisiCalc, an early spreadsheet tool

Finance teams weren't the only ones taking advantage of this new technology. Spreadsheets didn't just deliver process efficiency; the flexibility they provided was leveraged by a new audience of managers, HR teams, supply chain analysts, marketing executives, and almost every other function you can think of within a commercial organization.

Since then, the pace of change has been relentless and spreadsheet tools have become ubiquitous. If you have a computer, it's safe to say you've seen, if not used, a spreadsheet tool. It is estimated that up to two billion people use spreadsheet tools like Excel and Google Sheets every day.

The Ubiquity of Excel

Very quickly, spreadsheet tools proliferated: SuperCalc, Lotus 1-2-3, Multiplan, and many other vendors drove development throughout the 1980s, and innovation happened fast. Users were able to write more complex calculations, the UIs became more sophisticated, and features were introduced to build charts and graphs natively within the application.

When Excel started to gain popularity in the late 1980s, it positioned itself as the most advanced spreadsheet tool available—a claim many people would still agree with well over 40 years later. Sticking with Excel for the moment, what does it do now that it didn't do then? The list is substantial, but some of the core features it provides now include the following:

- The ability to maintain multiple independent and dynamically referenceable sheets within a single file
- A robust and wide-ranging collection of functions, including a framework to write custom functions in Visual Basic for Applications (VBA) to extend functionality and integrate with other third-party systems

- Integration features to obtain data from a wide variety of sources, like relational databases
- Sophisticated data modeling, query editing, and transformation features
- Math and trigonometry functions, along with built-in statistical modeling and forecasting tools
- A large range of sophisticated and customizable charts and graphs
- Capable online versions to allow for collaboration and version control
- Lots of options for exporting delimited data for use in other tools

This would be a sensible list of criteria to use when evaluating an analytics platform, so it's clear that Excel *can* demonstrably fulfill the function of an analytics platform. In fact, thousands of organizations around the world are using Excel as their sole platform for data orchestration and analysis right now, even if they don't know it.

Excel is so ubiquitous and feature-rich that it presents a path of least resistance to organizations faced with data and analytics requirements. In many cases, organizations have already paid for Excel as part of an existing Microsoft purchase, so they've already got the software—a big hurdle to overcome. And it provides a near-perfect fit for so many day-to-day challenges:

I need somewhere to store our monthly finance records.
Excel isn't necessarily a perfect solution for storing data, but with careful management it's a great fit for archiving lots of row-level data for future analysis.

I need to import some third-party data I found on the web and prepare it for analysis.
You're already familiar with the way Excel works, so you can just paste the data into a sheet and start working on it.

I have to build a chart for the weekly sales presentation.
You can build the chart you need in a couple of clicks, complete with drop shadows and gradient fills—which everyone loves, right?

I need to do a quick and dirty budget balance for the next staff meeting.
Excel's here; why not just use that? Basic formulas are easy to write, and you can send the file straight to your manager for approval.

The fact that Excel is such a good fit for these kinds of challenges has cemented its position as the default choice for a data and analytics platform in many organizations, but it's not necessarily the *right* choice.

What Excel Doesn't Do

The sheer scale of data challenges facing many organizations today means that a true analytics platform needs to provide far more robust controls over the way data is shared and consumed by users. The following sections explore a few ways in which Excel and similar spreadsheet tools don't meet the requirements of a true analytics platform.

 It's worth noting that many acquisition and merger strategies specifically include audit-style exercises that require companies to formally demonstrate data and analytics capabilities in many of the following areas to be considered "data mature."

Controlling the proliferation of content

Taylor works in a large recycling plant. Her daily responsibilities include downloading processing data from the plant management software and aggregating minute-level data to create KPIs, which she then sends to her manager. Every day, she saves a "work in progress" version on her local computer, then a final version. Sometimes, she creates a *really* final version after correcting mistakes. She emails copies of all these files to her manager, who saves them on their local computer.

Figure 8-8 shows a somewhat contrived example of this. We've all done it, and it's not just endemic to Excel. However, it does illustrate one of the major headaches of using completely democratized software to manage data. In Taylor's example, there are at least four or five files created *every workday* (assuming neither Taylor nor her manager distributes copies to anyone else), named in arbitrary ways and containing similar data. That's over a thousand files a year, distributed across various local computers, network storage locations, and internal mailboxes.

Name	Type	Size
Sept 23 raw data - Copy.csv	Microsoft Excel Comma Separated Values File	7 KB
Sept 23 raw data.xlsx	Microsoft Excel Worksheet	7 KB
Sept 2023 FINAL v2.xlsx	Microsoft Excel Worksheet	7 KB
Sept 2023 FINAL.xlsx	Microsoft Excel Worksheet	7 KB
Sept 2023 in progerss.xlsx	Microsoft Excel Worksheet	7 KB
Sept 2023 in progress - Copy.xlsx	Microsoft Excel Worksheet	7 KB
Sept 2023 Marks v.1.xlsx	Microsoft Excel Worksheet	7 KB

Desktop > Q4 reporting

Figure 8-8. An example of duplicate reporting content

Now, imagine a scenario where an external auditor asks for the last year's worth of data. Taylor will have a *lot* of work to do. Even worse, imagine a scenario where an external auditor asks the company to validate that a single source of accurate processing data is stored only in one secure location. Taylor's manager now has a lot of work to do!

This is the problem with proliferation of content; once it's permitted, it's almost impossible to control and very difficult to refactor.

Ability to support computation on large volumes of data

As of the time of writing, Excel can handle 1,048,576 rows and 16,384 columns in a single sheet. That (need it be said?) is a *big* spreadsheet. But in the real world most users are likely to encounter performance problems using Excel with far fewer rows, especially once the data needs to be manipulated and formulas computed.

The general complexity and volume of data extracted from CRM/ERP systems is ever-increasing, and while having to manipulate or otherwise work with million-row datasets seems unlikely, it's far more common than many organizations realize, especially when data is being manually integrated from multiple sources.

To handle the manipulation and transformation of datasets this large, you really need to look toward dedicated database solutions.

Security and authorization

One of the most crucial aspects of any data and analytics solution, a scalable security and governance strategy, is very difficult to implement reliably on top of a tool like Excel.

We talked in depth about what an effective governance and compliance solution looks like in Chapter 7, and if you review that chapter with Excel in mind, you'll come to an obvious conclusion: almost none of the core governance principles can be effectively implemented if Excel is considered to be the sole analytics platform, and certainly not without leveraging many costly additional external services to enforce even basic principles.

Sharing and embedding

Last, but by no means least, a true analytics platform depends on the ability to share content with users in a way that doesn't conflict with or break any already established governance principles or lead to content proliferation. A free-for-all distribution without any form of control is clearly undesirable, but Excel doesn't have a centralized model for sharing content outside of its own Microsoft-powered platform, and although it's possible to embed Excel documents hosted on third-party platforms, there's no inherent ability to control or otherwise federate access to that content within Excel itself.

To put it another way, if you wanted to embed Excel content in your own website or application, you're going to have challenges that simply don't exist with many dedicated data and analytics platforms.

Almost an Answer

Hopefully you can see why the question "Are spreadsheets analytics platforms?" isn't quite as straightforward as it seems, and your answer will undoubtedly vary depending on the ways you currently use spreadsheets and what your organization's relationship with data will look like in the future.

However, a reasonable statement to make would be as follows:

> Spreadsheet tools aren't inherently suited to be used as analytics platforms, but their level of adoption and their powerful and well-understood features make them an integral part of many analytics solutions.

Fortunately, the world of spreadsheet tools is no longer limited to monolithic, client-based applications like Excel. New highly focused, SaaS-based offerings are now bridging the gap between democratic access to data and tight governance in innovative ways. In addition, some tools have very interesting potential for embedded use cases.

Beyond Excel

While Excel has maintained its position as the most popular spreadsheet tool, the broader landscape of spreadsheet tools has hugely diversified. We're now seeing predominantly SaaS-based products gain traction, some of which focus on addressing very specific business challenges, like project management or survey capture.

SaaS generally provides more flexibility for integration, but of particular interest to us from an embedded analytics perspective is the use of these tools (and native tables) in a relatively new type of interactive collaborative development tool: the browser-based, computational notebook.

Let's explore a few of these categories, both old and new.

Simple Reporting and Analytics

Many vendors offer traditional spreadsheet tools that are geared toward supporting basic reporting analytics, and some of these tools leverage the fact that legacy tools like Excel are likely to remain the *source* for existing reporting data.

For example, GRID (*https://oreil.ly/pIuzU*) allows users to connect to existing data in Excel and then create rich, interactive visualizations from the data, which can be shared with other users and include narrative and contextual feedback, like comments. GRID has its own native spreadsheet editor, but the product is primarily positioned to fulfill a common use case: the presentation of, and collaboration around, analytics (something Excel does not natively provide).

Comparably, Google Sheets is a more generalized online spreadsheet tool that leverages Google's robust app ecosystem to provide rich collaboration capabilities, not just within Sheets, but also across other products in Google Workspace, like Slides and Docs.

Tools like these trade heavily on the user's familiarity with traditional spreadsheet concepts, like writing calculations, formatting, and the general "flow" of working with data: copying and pasting content, creating summary or aggregated tables, etc. As such, they're often an appropriate choice if you're considering embedded table content in your analytics solutions.

Figure 8-9 uses the same table we used in our examples earlier in the chapter. In this case, we've created a Google Sheet to contain the data in question and embedded it in a web page using the native iframe-based sharing capabilities in Google Sheets. You can imagine how a web page could easily be created that embeds several sheets containing both tables and charts, all potentially generated by the same tool.

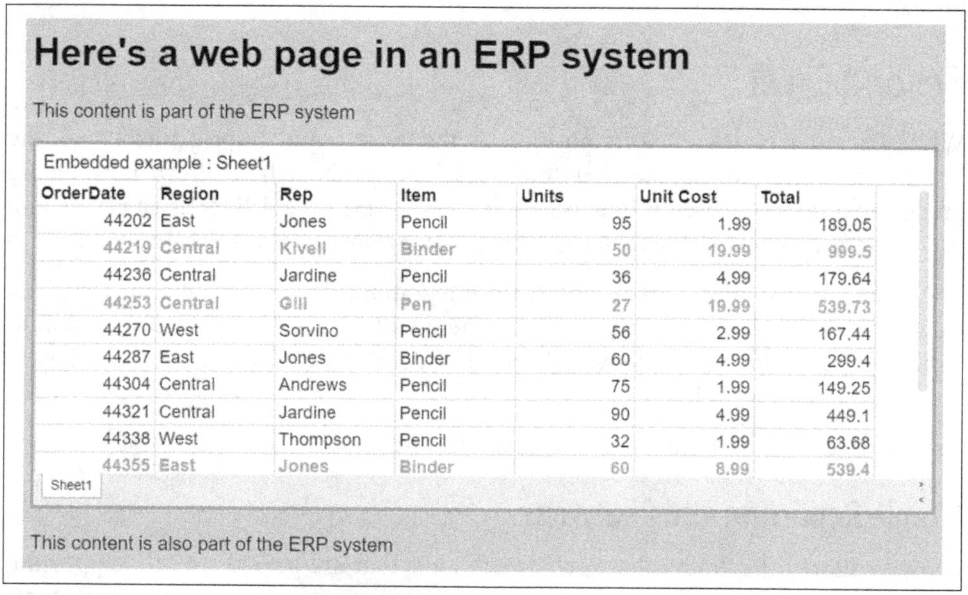

Here's a web page in an ERP system

This content is part of the ERP system

Embedded example : Sheet1

OrderDate	Region	Rep	Item	Units	Unit Cost	Total
44202	East	Jones	Pencil	95	1.99	189.05
44219	Central	Kivell	Binder	50	19.99	999.5
44236	Central	Jardine	Pencil	36	4.99	179.64
44253	Central	Gill	Pen	27	19.99	539.73
44270	West	Sorvino	Pencil	56	2.99	167.44
44287	East	Jones	Binder	60	4.99	299.4
44304	Central	Andrews	Pencil	75	1.99	149.25
44321	Central	Jardine	Pencil	90	4.99	449.1
44338	West	Thompson	Pencil	32	1.99	63.68
44355	East	Jones	Binder	60	8.99	539.4

Sheet1

This content is also part of the ERP system

Figure 8-9. An iframe in a web page containing an embedded Google Sheet

This is a very simplistic example, with a publicly available Google Sheet. Recall that security and authorization are critical components of a true analytics platform and should be considered a default requirement if your use case requires anything other than unrestricted access to content.

Integration and Collaboration

We've touched on the idea of collaboration being a potentially valuable feature for a spreadsheet tool. Some vendors have taken this concept much further to build spreadsheet-based products that use tables as a central repository for powerful collaboration and integration use cases. This repeatable and reusable "framework" approach provides flexibility: interfaces can be used to create intuitive and visual ways for data to be captured, forms to be created, projects to be tracked, and data to be analyzed.

Additionally, many of the tools in this category, like Airtable (*https://oreil.ly/2ykAQ*), have connectors for other common productivity tools, which can be used to move information between the spreadsheet tool and other services. What does this mean in practice?

- Content from other applications, such as visual whiteboarding platforms, can be displayed alongside related tables in the tool.
- Notifications can be sent from the tool to communication platforms like Slack and Microsoft Teams when tables or user-facing interfaces are updated.
- CRM or ERP tools can be updated directly when statuses are updated in the tool.

The possibilities are endless, and tools in this category often present a compelling and cost-effective option for organizations seeking to solve operational challenges.

Project Management and Workflow

Spreadsheet concepts lend themselves well to project management methodologies. Tasks with any number of attributes (duration, date, status, complexity, etc.) are a natural fit for tables, and cell formatting makes pseudo-Gantt charts easy to create and maintain. Vendors have sought to take advantage of this to create tools such as Smartsheet (*https://oreil.ly/sm8mU*) and monday.com that provide a broad range of features to support typical management and workflow-based requirements like task management, lead management, onboarding, contact management, and campaign management. It's a rich seam to mine for vendors because the features to support all these use cases can all be derived from the basic concept of storing data in the form of a spreadsheet.

Computational Notebooks

Potentially one of the most interesting ways that table-based data can be used in an embedded analytics context is the relatively recent concept of the computational notebook. In basic terms, a *computational notebook* (or just "notebook" for the purposes of this chapter) is a web-based environment where documents can be created that contain text and rich media alongside defined blocks that can contain code, visual analytics, mathematical representations, and, of course, tables.

Notebooks gained popularity because they very effectively combine core integrated development environment (IDE) concepts, like the ability to write, edit, debug, and run code, with collaborative and narrative concepts, like explaining what the code does (with text) and visualizing the results (with embedded tables and visual analytics). A notebook becomes a low-dependency, self-contained interactive environment for developing code, which is perfect for team-based code development, data science, and analytics.

Figure 8-10 shows a basic example of a notebook hosted on Google's collaborative notebook platform, Colaboratory (*https://oreil.ly/KHzwP*), a great resource for those who want to experiment with notebooks. Our notebook includes formatted commentary, snippets of code that can be executed in real time, and the results of the executed code: an embedded, interactive table.

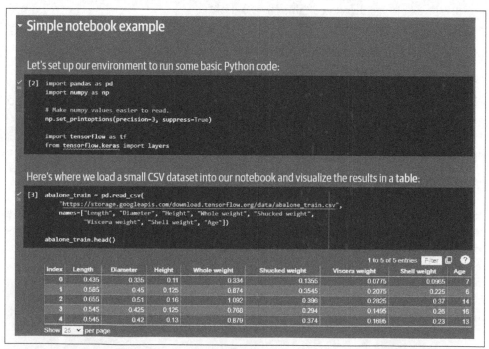

Figure 8-10. A sample computational notebook

Behind the scenes, a notebook is a document containing code, text, and rich media that uses a computational component called the *kernel* to execute any code and integration processes that may be included in the document. It's typical for the notebook platform and kernel to be hosted on a cloud services provider like Amazon Web Services (AWS) or Azure, so the kernel can leverage scalable compute resources to handle the code execution. This makes notebooks a compelling solution for computationally intensive AI and machine learning projects, enabling an explanation of what you're doing to be presented alongside code (and the results of that code), which can be executed in real time.

 One inevitable consequence of product diversification is that terminology and nomenclature become more complex. Vendors seek to differentiate their product features by introducing completely new terms that represent similar things, and a great deal of time in product evaluation projects can be spent simply learning what these new terms represent. It can feel like an unproductive effort, but it's important to do in order to meaningfully compare features.

Putting Spreadsheets in Context

Should you consider spreadsheet tools and tables as embeddable objects that can add value to your solution? Unequivocally, yes. But there are several caveats.

Choose the Spreadsheet Tool Carefully

If you've decided that your embedded analytics solution requires tables for a legitimate reason, and you believe they will add value or improve the user experience, pay careful attention to the considerations we discussed at the start of this chapter. Embedding tables from traditional spreadsheet tools (like Excel) will potentially break defined governance principles, open up security risks, and be far more difficult to manage in comparison to embedded visual analytics objects served up from a dedicated visual analytics platform.

Don't Break the Paradigm of Visual Analytics

This might be a more diplomatic way of saying "don't be lazy." Visual analytics exist because they leverage humans' ancient selection, enumeration, and pattern recognition capabilities to communicate insight as effectively as possible. If you're considering embedding a table, ask yourself whether it is *definitively* the best way to communicate and present data for the purpose in question. If not, then reverting to an appropriate chart or graph (or KPI) may be a better choice, irrespective of the features and functionality the spreadsheet tool may provide.

Pursue Consistent Methods for Interaction Where Possible

In many cases (as with the concept of computational notebooks), the mechanism or spreadsheet tool being used to generate the table is going to be different from the tool used to generate visual charts. For example, you may embed a ThoughtSpot live-board in a solution alongside a table generated by Airtable—two completely different software solutions. The methods for interacting with those embedded elements are, naturally, going to be different. Drilling down may require slightly different processes in each tool, and certain interaction methods, like right-clicking, may not work in both tools.

To an extent, this is unavoidable (and perhaps expected by users), but nonetheless it's important to think carefully about how users will manage and understand the interaction options available to them when tools from multiple vendors are used.

Consider Highly Targeted Use Cases for Tables

At the start of this chapter, we briefly mentioned the common pattern of users who simply want to download or export delimited data from an embedded system. Again, there's a case to be made here that appropriate use of visual analytics may negate the requirement to export in the first place. After all, if the user wants to download the data to build a chart in Excel, why not build an embedded interactive version of that chart and keep the user in the system?

However, there are legitimate reasons for users needing to download data. They might have to conduct analyses that aren't possible in the embedded system they're using. They might be required to upload the data to a third-party system as part of their own workflow. Or, in the case of external-facing or monetized embedded analytics solutions, there may be a contractual requirement to make the data available.

In any of these cases, tables perform a valuable role in your embedded solution: previewing data for exporting and giving the user the ability to refine and otherwise control what eventually makes it into the downloaded file.

Figure 8-11 shows a great example of this. Tableau can preview data used in a particular chart or view and download the underlying data (assuming the user has the appropriate permissions). In this case, the user is shown a table representing the data they're going to download, with the ability to preview a selected number of rows and show or hide columns that may not be used in the chart itself. This is a good user experience, and a perfect example of how tables can be used to add value to an embedded experience.

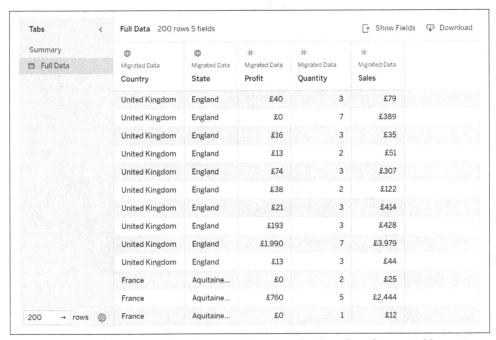

Figure 8-11. A table presented to the user when downloading data from a Tableau view

Conclusion

Spreadsheet tools are no longer just for creating tables, and users have access to an enormous range of tools, platforms, and nascent technologies based on the concept of storing data in rows and columns. This doesn't necessarily mean that tables are *needed* to form part of an effective embedded analytics solution, but with careful consideration and tool selection, embedding tabular content to provide additional context can provide users with options they expect (like downloading and exporting data). Providing a guided analytic experience is something that any solution architect should explore.

CHAPTER 9

Data Science, Machine Learning, and Embedded Analytics

In this chapter, we're going to explore the intersection between embedded analytics, data science, and machine learning (ML). This chapter is aimed particularly at decision-makers considering the application of data science and machine learning to provide additional value to existing business processes and embedded applications. We'll also make the case that context and "storytelling" around data science and machine learning is arguably just as important as the application of the processes themselves.

This is a complex topic, so for the sake of simplicity, we're going to intentionally blur the boundaries between the specific fields of data science and machine learning and refer generally instead to DSML. In the real world, many vendor tools, platforms, and methodologies use features from both disciplines, and against the backdrop of general analytics, it's safe to say these terms (and many others, like artificial intelligence and predictive analytics) are often used interchangeably.

DSML in Practice

So, what does DSML encapsulate beyond the traditional analytics we've discussed so far? Typically, a mature organization where data analytics is well practiced may demonstrate capabilities in one or more of the following areas:

- The active use of sophisticated statistical or probability-based methods to enrich or derive insight from data and support decision making

- The use of languages like Python and R for transformation, preparation, and analysis of data, instead of low- or no-code visual analytics tools like Tableau, Power BI, or Sisense

- Less commonly, the advanced use of SQL data definition language (DDL) and DML commands to conduct DSML on data directly in a relational database

- The application of easily scalable SaaS DSML services provided by cloud platform providers, like Amazon SageMaker or Azure Machine Learning Studio

- General expertise in machine learning operations (MLOps) practices to deploy, maintain, and manage production ML models within a dedicated team

We'll talk about the real-world applications for some of these capabilities and how they can both support and drive effective embedded analytics solutions later in this chapter, but for now let's explore a fundamental consideration for any organization approaching DSML.

DSML Is Hard

If you're familiar with the concept of analytics maturity, where various stages of maturity are plotted on a graph to indicate progression from basic descriptive analytics through to prescriptive analytics, you may already be aware that most, if not all, of the capabilities and skillsets we just discussed fall into the high difficulty/high value quadrant.

Figure 9-1 shows a version of the analytics maturity model illustrating where DSML is commonly used (or proposed) for predictive and prescriptive analytics purposes.

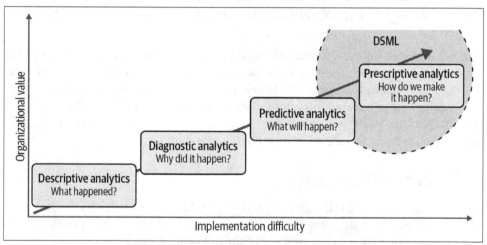

Figure 9-1. An illustration of the ubiquitous analytics maturity concept

DSML can be costly and difficult to implement effectively, but it also can provide transformative value for organizations when it's done properly. However, here's where we need to consider one of the most challenging issues: how to engage with and explain DSML concepts and processes to nontechnical stakeholders.

The Power of Storytelling

Getting buy-in for traditional analytics projects is much easier than it used to be. Organizations don't need to be convinced of the enormous value locked up in reporting data anymore. There's a huge range of highly effective and intuitive analytics tools and products available to suit every budget, and developing basic analytics capabilities is within reach of almost any organization.

However, when it comes to moving beyond basic analytics into the DSML-driven world of predictive and prescriptive analytics, it gets much trickier. As we've touched on, in addition to core analytics knowledge, DSML involves highly technical concepts, an understanding of basic statistics and machine learning modeling (which is not a component of most real-world traditional analytics), and sophisticated and costly technology.

It's also crucial to have the resources to translate tangible organizational requirements into applicable DSML projects and to be able to effectively communicate the value of the results back to the organization through "storytelling." This is where many DSML projects fail before they've even begun.

When Things Go Wrong

Let's illustrate the impact storytelling can have (or not) with a real-world example.

A professional football organization is developing its media campaign to promote an upcoming league tournament, and after a selection process lasting many months, a relatively small advertising agency with a heavy tech focus has been picked to run the campaign. It's an eight-figure budget, and the contract represents financial security for the agency for the next two years. In other words, it's a big deal.

The agency knows it has to do something different: showcase the tournament, as well as understand what fans want to see, what moments are important to them, and why they follow the game. This will define the content and the direction the campaign takes. The idea gains traction, and because the agency is tech-focused, it decides to use a technique called *network science* to better understand how fans interact with each other. The agency distills the project down to a single question: what brings fans together?

Irrespective of their preferred teams, fans unite over historical events: great games, controversial games, final-deciding penalties. The "highlights of football" are where the universal interaction between fans happens.

So, the agency decides that a campaign focusing on these highlight moments is the answer. It determines what these moments are and the sentiments around them by using DSML—specifically, an application of graph theory and network science—to evaluate the millions of interactions of fans on social media.

However, network science is complicated. No problem: the agency sends in its campaign manager and data scientist to pitch the idea to the football executives. The data scientist excitedly explains how *edges*, *nodes*, *weighting*, *network-based*, and *self-based properties* will be used in Python's NetworkX package to determine *centrality measures* like *closeness* and *betweenness*. He shows a slide, like the example in Figure 9-2. He's excited. Surely the executives will be impressed!

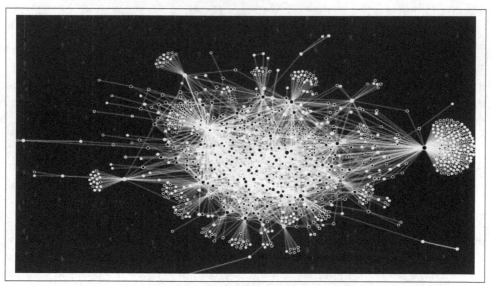

Figure 9-2. A visualization of a network graph

Unfortunately, the data scientist's presentation is met with silence, and after an excruciating few seconds, one exec quietly says, "I think we'd better talk to your boss, if that's OK. That's all for now." Confused and crestfallen, the data scientist leaves the room.

The execs tell the campaign manager in no uncertain terms that the proposal is, frankly, incomprehensible. Meaningless, they say. Perhaps they should rethink the contract. Can't the agency explain in simple terms what the proposal *actually is*?

The campaign manager, starting to panic, goes back to basics: "OK. Hear me out. We're going to apply cutting-edge data science techniques to find out exactly what fans of opposing teams talk about with each other on social media. What they agree on, what they disagree on, the things that truly unite them. And then we're going to craft the most beautiful, soul-stirring TV campaign around these moments that you've ever seen. And we know it'll resonate with fans, because that's what the science tells us."

The response is immediate. Eyes light up as the execs suddenly understand why the agency wants to do all this fancy DSML stuff. It'll be revolutionary, they think. Success is assured! Confidence restored, the campaign manager and the (now slightly more cheerful) data scientist return to base with the contract safely in hand.

This is a contrived story, but hopefully it serves to reiterate the point we made earlier: it's vital not only to have the resources to translate organizational requirements into applicable DSML projects, but also to be able to effectively communicate the value of the results back to the organization. At the start of the story, the agency was confident that the sheer weight of technical expertise was all that was needed to demonstrate the value of its idea, when in fact, simple and effective storytelling was needed to explain the "why" of the proposal.

 If you're interested in network graph theory, *Towards Data Science* has some great resources available online, specifically "Visualizing Networks in Python" (*https://oreil.ly/AnM89*), which works through various options for visualizing networks in the same way we talked about in our story.

So, what relevance does this have for embedded analytics? Consider this: embedding analytics objects derived from DSML in a native application or interface provides you with a perfect mechanism to provide *context* about the value of DSML. Let's explore what that means.

The DSML-Driven Call Center

To help explain how some of the key DSML concepts can be applied in a real-world scenario that's slightly less complex that our network graph use case, we're going to explore a typical use of DSML that is common in call centers and other point-of-sale environments: propensity modeling. Just as importantly, we'll also explain how end users interact with the solution and use embedded analytics to understand *context* and *value* without needing to understand anything about DSML.

Propensity Modeling

At a very high level, *propensity modeling* is simply the process of using historical data (the very same data often used for descriptive analytics) to predict the likelihood of certain events happening in the future (an application of predictive analytics). Let's look at a real-world example using an imaginary call center.

Our call center has made millions of B2B sales calls over the last few years. Every call has a corresponding row in a database that includes details of the customer (organization, position, name, gender, address, details of previous purchases, etc.) and details of the call itself (duration, call handler, team, date and time, script, etc.).

Using the customer's address to link to other sources containing geographic data, the row also includes some third-party demographic data about the affluence and economic status of the area where the customer is located. The row for a single call might contain hundreds of columns, all holding potentially useful data. However, there's one column that's very important for our example. It's called "sold" and contains either a 1 (indicating that the call resulted in a sale) or a 0 (indicating that it did not).

The simple metric that this column drives is the *conversion rate* for our call center: the percentage of calls that lead to a sale. Maximizing this rate is key. So, how do we do that? Well, let's take a step out of the details for a minute and think about some of the aspects of the call center we might change to boost conversion:

- The call handlers are provided with a *list of new customers to call* each day. We can control which customers are on this list.

- Call handlers are *organized into teams* based on individual performance. We can control which teams call customers on which lists.

- There are *different scripts* available for call handlers to use. We can dictate which script to use.

Let's start by focusing on the first point. The call center has data about millions of potential customers they can call. If we can ensure that we call only those customers who are likely to make a purchase, we're going to increase our conversion rate. This is where DSML comes in.

Training a Model

The basic challenge is this: given details about a new potential customer, we need to determine if they're likely to make a purchase or not. Using DSML, we can use historical data to train a machine learning model to predict this for us.

In simple terms, we do this by preparing the data, utilizing an ML service, and training and testing a model, as discussed in the following sections.

Preparing the data

First, we take our historical data and tidy it up. There's almost always some issue with incomplete data, and before any ML processes are applied it's a good idea to do some basic cleansing and preparation of the data, such as setting data types correctly. We might also create new calculations that may be useful to train our model, such as determining the age of a contact (in years) using their date of birth.

Most importantly, we need to make sure that the "sold" column is accurately and consistently stored, because this is the value we want to predict.

Utilizing an ML service

Next, we pass this data into an ML service—Microsoft's Azure ML Studio, for example. We want to train a classification model using our historical data. Or, to put it in simple terms, we want the model to find out *what it is* about customers that makes them likely to make a purchase. We know lots about our customers; there may be combinations of these aspects (or "features" as they're called in DSML) that make a particular customer likely to buy something.

For example, maybe male contacts with a lifetime value (LTV) of over $34,000 who have not made a purchase in the last six months, and who have moved from a more affluent area to a less affluent area in the last three years, are more likely to make a purchase than other contacts. There are millions of customers in our dataset, and there are hundreds of features (organization, gender, location, demographics, etc.), so it's way beyond the capability of humans to determine exactly what it is that leads a customer to make a purchase. There might be *billions* of potential combinations of features.

ML has no such issues with the scale of a challenge like this, and depending on the available compute resources, it can often determine results in minutes.

Training and testing a model

We tell our ML model that we want to train it to predict the value of our "sold" column. It iterates through our dataset, testing millions of feature combinations to determine which combinations are associated with an increased likelihood to purchase. These features are assigned weights according to how much they contribute to the likelihood, and the model is run again, each time predicting what the value of the "sold" column is with either a 1 or a 0. The model's efficacy can be tested by comparing the predicted results with the actual results stored in the historical data, and from this the overall accuracy of our model is scored.

The details and theory behind the supervised machine learning model we're using in this example (a basic binary classification model) are out of scope for this book. A wide range of models are provided as services by most cloud platforms, like AWS and Azure, and dedicated data science tools, like Dataiku. In many cases, little experience is required to implement these models, although expertise *is* required for feature engineering, training, and interpreting the results of models.

In our imaginary case, after training and testing our model and experimenting with different features and parameters, we arrive at a model that can predict the likelihood of conversion (based on historical data) with 84% accuracy. This is a fantastic result and well within the remit of what modern DSML models can predict given appropriate data.

It's time to productionize our model.

Putting It into Practice

We can now solve the problem of which customers to call. In the customer service system, every time a customer record is loaded, we run that record through our ML model, which instantly returns a prediction of their likelihood to buy. These records can be provided to the call handlers, and the rest discarded.

Straightforward applications of DSML like this are happening in thousands of call centers across the world right now, and the results can be transformative. However, we can leverage the value of this approach in more nuanced ways:

- First, remember that call handlers in our example are organized into teams based on their performance. Descriptive data has shown that for a given customer, veteran, high-performing teams are more likely to elicit a sale than less experienced, low-performing teams.

- Similarly, remember that different scripts are used in the actual conversations, promoting certain products or discounts accordingly. These scripts have an impact on conversion, too. Both of these aspects can be used as features to train a new multiclassification ML model, with the idea that different combinations of scripts and teams may also influence conversion rate.

Figure 9-3 shows a very simplistic relational diagram describing this slightly more advanced implementation. Using a model trained not only to predict the likelihood of a sale, but also the most appropriate team and script (a multiclass classification model), we can discard contacts that are unlikely to convert, but then ensure we provide the remaining contacts to the best team using the best script to further maximize our chances of a sale.

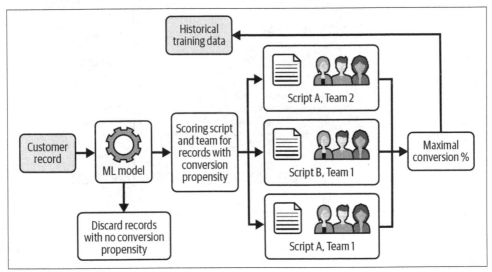

Figure 9-3. An illustration of our DSML model in production

Closing the Loop

Let's explore what the end user experience looks like for a manager in our call center. The core concept is that we're using embedded analytics objects to provide teams with all the supporting information they need to engage with their customers. Embedded analytics has also provided them with DSML-derived prescriptive intelligence to maximize the likelihood of a sale.

Figure 9-4 shows an imaginary call management system screen, from the point of view of a call center manager responsible for monitoring daily team performance and allocating customer contacts to teams to call.

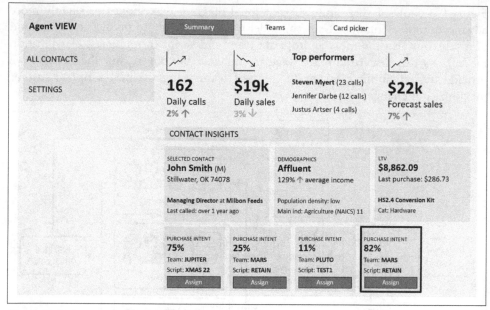

Figure 9-4. An example of a call management system page

This single view embeds several valuable analytics objects, shown from top to bottom:

- Visual descriptive analytics KPIs based on call data being captured in the call center during the day

- Basic contact details derived from the contacts database, allowing the call handler to engage with the customer and understand the nature of their previous calls and purchases

- Augmented demographics data based on contact location, further informing the call handler about attributes that might be useful in the sales process

- Lifetime value insights for the contact, based on previous purchase history

- DSML-derived prescriptive data (from our previous example) about the best combination of team and script to use to maximize the likelihood of a sale, along with a simple one-click mechanism to "assign" the contact to a specific team

- A predictive forecast sales value based on the daily sales figure and the conversion likelihood of calls being passed to the team

This is a great example of an embedded solution providing *context* and illustrating the *value* of data derived by (potentially) highly complex analytical and DSML work-flows without end users needing any expertise or technical knowledge.

To add some additional context for this idea of "closing the loop," Figure 9-5 shows an actual screenshot of an embedded element generated by Salesforce, included within a Tableau dashboard (which could also be embedded in a target application or web page).

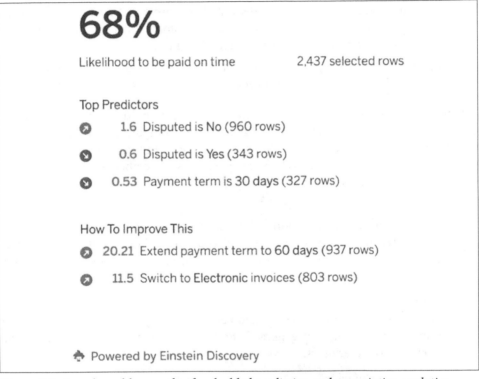

Figure 9-5. A real-world example of embedded predictive and prescriptive analytics

This example not only provides predictive analytics (the percentage likelihood of an account paying on time), but prescriptive analytics (the recommended action to increase this likelihood) that can be acted upon by our users.

This is a great example of how powerful the combination of embedded analytics and DSML-generated insights can be.

Other Typical Use Cases

Our examples have explored one potential way to push DSML-driven insights into an embedded system. The way in which the DSML model *itself* is developed and deployed could be handled in a variety of ways:

- Pure code developed and orchestrated by cloud platform services (like lambda functions) that integrate directly with data and target systems
- Models developed and trained in dedicated platforms and deployed within the "walled garden" of a particular vendor (like Salesforce Einstein Discovery) or as an addressable service created in a tool like Dataiku
- Industry- or vertical-specific services designed solely to handle common use cases (like default predication, conversion attribution, or credit card fraud)

Whatever method is used to develop, train, and deploy models, the use of DSML now accounts for a significant percentage of overall compute use within the major cloud computing providers like AWS, Azure, and GCP, and new use cases are being developed every day. Of specific relevance to analytics and embedded applications are examples like the following:

Customer journey optimization
Customer journey optimization (as illustrated in our call center example) uses DSML to recommend or enact the most appropriate next action in a customer journey—that is, the one that has the highest likelihood of resulting in a desired action, like a sale.

Content curation
Content curation is often used to automatically display content on a website (or within an application) that generates the highest level of engagement, based on the behavior of other users.

Recommendation engines
Recommendation engines use DSML to suggest appropriate products to users based on their purchasing history, engagement patterns of other users, stock availability, and pricing strategies.

Demand and pricing forecasting models
Demand and pricing forecasting models continuously optimize supply chain operations to ensure that appropriate stock volumes are available, based on historical trading conditions, market fluctuations, and other features.

Increasingly, DSML is also used to optimize the user experience within applications and systems themselves, which is of particular benefit to applications where user interaction is something that can be optimized for purchasing paths. This is manifest in online retailers (such as Amazon) that use DSML to ensure query results "learn" from the customer's immediate search history.

The Rise of Generative Language Services

Given when this book was written (in early 2023), it would be remiss to not at least mention the exploding popularity and potential of highly sophisticated generative natural language processing and generation (NLP/NLG) tools like GPT-4. While not strictly in the scope of embedded analytics in the sense that we've been discussing, it's inevitable that AI-driven natural language systems will see increasing adoption in many of the use cases we've explored in this chapter.

Generative language services like GPT-4 are essentially highly sophisticated deep learning models that have been trained using enormous quantities of textual data. Given some input text from a user—a question or a request, for example—a language model (LM) determines the most likely sequence of words to serve as a response. The responses can be used not only for straightforward question answering and basic information retrieval purposes, but also for much more complex (and surprising) applications like writing working code and poetry!

As an example of how powerful these services can be, consider the following input and output generated using GPT-4:

> **Prompt:** My monthly product sales are declining. Provide me with five factors that could be causes.
>
> **Response:** If your monthly product sales are declining, there could be a variety of factors at play. Here are five possible causes:
>
> Competition: Increased competition in the market could be affecting your sales.
>
> Economic factors: Changes in the overall economy, such as a recession or a decrease in consumer spending, could be impacting your sales.
>
> Product quality: A decline in the quality of your product could be affecting customer satisfaction and leading to a decrease in sales.
>
> Marketing strategies: Ineffective marketing strategies, or a shift in consumer preferences, could be affecting your sales.
>
> Supply chain disruptions: Issues with your supply chain, such as production delays or increased costs, could be affecting your ability to meet customer demand and resulting in a decrease in sales.

This is a compelling example. You can imagine a sales manager about to hold a meeting to address the declining sales issue confidently using these insights to direct some investigation.

It doesn't take much of a leap to see the potential these services have for analytical use cases: a single search-based interface that can respond immediately to natural language questions and integrate data-driven results into natural language output that, in many cases, is indistinguishable from user-created output. Vendors like ThoughtSpot and Veezoo are already developing products in this area, eschewing traditional dashboard creation in favor of search-based natural language analytics.

It's the authors' considered opinion that generative language services will dramatically transform the analytics landscape in the next few years. It's also worth pointing out that (aside from the preceding example) no GPT-4 results have been used in the creation of this book!

Conclusion

This chapter both explained and explored the value that DSML-driven analytics can have within the context of embedded solutions. And, if you're considering DSML as a component of your own analytics solution, hopefully we've clarified that although data science ability is critical, it's also very important to have capable people involved whose role is to translate organizational requirements and effectively communicate the value of the results back to the organization.

In the next chapter, we're going to talk about bringing everything we've learned so far together and explore ways in which analytics solutions can become commercially viable products in their own right.

CHAPTER 10

Analytics as a Line of Business

We began this book with a simple claim: every business today is a data business. From there, it was a short step to say that every business needs to be an analytic business to get the best from its data. For many companies, this need to be analytical represents a challenge. They may not have the infrastructure or the skills to define and build the analytics they need. They may not have the budget and resources, or even if they do, they may not be able to prioritize data analysis over other strategic plans.

For software vendors, this unmet demand is a significant commercial prospect. You are already building applications or services that your customers need: you can enhance your range of products by adding analytics as a feature, or even developing specialized analytics products that can stand on their own.

This potential is particularly potent for SaaS vendors. Buyers are used to SaaS products offering a relatively low cost, simple adoption, and continuously released updates. In this demanding and competitive environment, where is your additional value to come from?

We believe one of the clearest answers is to be found in the data you already manage. In this chapter, we will look beyond building analytics as a feature to see how you can deliver analytics as a product and therefore as a potential line of business.

Data as an Asset

We are probably all familiar with the phrase, *data is an asset*. In fact, it's a cliché of modern data management and analytics practice. It means, of course, that data has value. That value emerges from the way in which data allows businesses to gain insights into customer behavior, trends, and preferences. These insights can be used to inform decisions and strategies. Data also helps businesses identify opportunities to improve efficiency, manage costs, and increase profitability.

Sometimes that value can be realized directly through data monetization, In other words, datasets can simply be sold, such as through a data marketplace, data brokers, or data as a service. Additionally, data can be sold directly to customers or through a subscription-based business model. Data can also be packaged and sold as a product or as part of a larger service.

Of course, there are restrictions that we must be aware of. Legal and ethical restrictions are very important in this scenario. But still, a lot of companies have the ambition to see real value from their data assets.

Managing the Data Asset

If we seriously consider data to be a business asset, this implies more than the fact that data has value. Think of other assets of a business: buildings, equipment, stock in hand, and so on. They have value, but that value may diminish over time. The same is true of data. All these assets need to be managed carefully to retain as much value as possible.

For example, businesses should track and monitor their assets to ensure they know where they are, who has access to them, and how they are being used. This may include creating an inventory or catalog of all assets and setting up systems to monitor their use. It is also essential to ensure assets are properly secured to prevent theft or misuse.

Similarly, for data, data governance, data quality, and data security are not just good practices; they are necessary to maintain the value of this asset. If your data is to be an asset, there is work to be done!

Think of data assets as just the start of a path to value that can deliver new features, new products, and new lines of business. As an example, the London Stock Exchange in 2008 derived most of its business from trading and stocks. As shown in Figure 10-1, by 2018, the largest single component of its income—the value of which had quadrupled in that period—came from selling data. And the second largest component was derived from providing clearing services, which are data-driven services built around the trading technologies. In other words, in 10 years the London Stock Exchange had gone from being primarily a stock exchange to being primarily a data and technology company. Of course, it still has to be a stock exchange to generate the business that in turn generates the data, but its primary sources of income are now from data and analytics as a line of business.

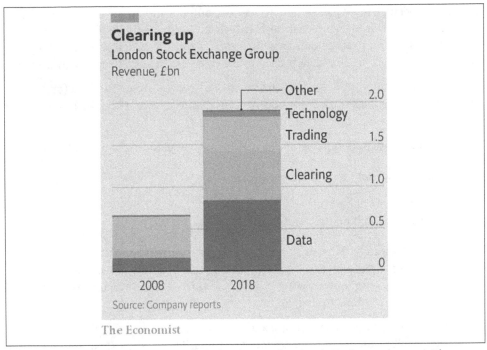

Figure 10-1. Data as a line of business for the London Stock Exchange (source: The Economist: https://oreil.ly/Z9q6l)

To be realistic, you won't always see the dramatic benefits that the London Stock Exchange experienced. Nevertheless, in this chapter, we want to set out a path that enables you to see real value from your data and analytics, especially in scenarios where you can embed analytics into applications that are already familiar to your customers.

One of the most effective ways to do this is to *productize* your data and analytics offerings—in short, to turn your data (and its analysis) from an asset into a product.

Data Products

Embedded analytics provides an excellent platform for building data products. For one thing, as we have described before, data on its own has limited value. Analysis, even just simple reporting or visualization, helps to make data more usable and valuable by enabling users to quickly identify patterns, trends, and correlations. By presenting data in a visual format, you enable users to more easily process and understand the information. Visualizations can also be used to highlight key findings, making them easier to remember and recall.

In addition, visualizing data can help to identify outliers and errors in the data, which can then be addressed before further analysis is conducted. Finally, visualizations can be used to communicate data insights more effectively to stakeholders and other users, helping to ensure that data is used in the most useful and effective way possible.

By providing this additional value, analytics as a new feature or module (or even as a new product) enables software vendors to upsell into new markets, including larger enterprises.

There are three integration patterns you can follow when adding value with analytics:

- Enhanced features for existing products
- New data and analytic modules
- New products built on data and analytics

In general, enhanced features are simply that: improvements to existing functionality made by adding some analytics capabilities. A simple example is embedding visualizations or reports within an existing page to provide clearer or more insightful help to a user making decisions in that context.

New modules may range from reports added as new tabs in an existing application to extensive visualization or machine learning features. The modular packaging of these features means that they can be deployed independently as add-ons to an existing product. As a result, they may be offered as options and even priced separately. (See the section "Pricing Embedded Analytics" on page 136 for more thoughts on this process.)

Finally, there is the possibility to create a new product, specifically providing specialized analytics, based on the operational data your existing product generates or collects. New products may have their own marketing and sales initiatives alongside their own product management, development, release, and support processes.

Documentation for Embedded Analytics

When extending an existing product with embedded analytics or creating an entire new module or SKU, it is important to keep the new documentation as consistent as possible with the existing product documentation in terms of language, format, and structure. This helps with usability, training, and support.

Remembering that analytics are new capabilities for your users, keep it simple and straightforward, avoiding jargon and explaining new technical terms. Also incorporate visuals illustrating how the new interface features integrate with the existing product.

The following points will help with explaining specific data and analytic features:

Explain the purpose and benefits.
Clearly explain the purpose of the product and the benefits it provides for users.

Provide data definitions.
Define the data elements and metrics used in the product.

Give examples.
Provide examples of how the data and analytics can be used to solve real-world problems.

Describe the data sources.
Explain where the data was sourced from and any assumptions made about the data.

Show visualizations.
Provide visualizations of the data and analytics to help users understand what the product is doing.

Explain the algorithms.
Describe any algorithms used to generate the data and analytics.

Product Analytics for Embedded Analytics Technologies

When you embed analytics into an existing software product, users experience this new functionality as *your* enhancement and your new features, even if the analytics solution is running on a third-party platform. This is especially true if you have followed our advice on security, data access, and the user experience. The final application can be seamless.

Many software vendors use *product analytics* systems to instrument and monitor the use of their software by users. Product analytics helps vendors understand how people use their products. For example, at a high level, you can learn in detail how much time users spend with your software, which features they use most often, and even if there are features they start to use but struggle with. This knowledge can drive not only product design decisions, but also marketing and sales strategy.

Product analytics technologies generally come with an SDK used to develop applications built on the analytics platform. SDKs generally include libraries, code samples, documentation, and tools for debugging and testing.

It's important to understand that even for web-based products, these product analytics technologies are not the same as web analytics products such as Google Analytics.

Web analytics is the process of analyzing and interpreting the data collected from a website or web-based application. It involves collecting, measuring, and analyzing user interactions with a website to understand how it is being used and how visitors are engaging with it. This data can then be used to improve the user experience and optimize the site's performance.

Product analytics measures how people behave once they are inside your product and working with it. With product analytics, you can gain insights into how users are engaging with your product, identify areas of improvement, and measure the success of product updates. By tracking events and user activity, you can understand user journeys, demographic data, and more. You can also easily segment user data to gain more targeted insights. Many product analytics platforms additionally provide features such as A/B testing and cohort analysis, which enable you to make more informed decisions about your product.

A good embedded analytics platform may include some features similar to those used in product analytics. For example, you may be able to answer questions such as the following:

- How many users have discovered and are using the new report type we released in the latest version?
- Are users regularly creating certain self-service objects that we should build into the main product?
- Are there peak times during the day when users refresh and use particular dashboards? Can we optimize our refresh times (for better performance and to save users cloud costs) based on this information?

You can see how the answers to these questions could help you design new features, improve existing capabilities, and optimize performance.

If you already have a product analytics capability for the host application, you have a choice. You can use your current product analytics features to log some usage information from the embedded features, or you can use the logging capabilities of the embedded analytics components independently. Your choice will depend on how detailed you need this logging to be. Initially, you may be interested only in how many people use the embedded features and how often, in which case your existing product analytics will likely be good enough.

Self-Service as a Feature

No matter how thorough your understanding of customer requirements and how deep your vertical specialization, it is unlikely that you can deliver every feature and every insight that advanced users demand. Sometimes they may have their own data sources with new information, or they may want to build a new dashboard for a specific use case.

If users must request these features from their IT department, which must then request them from you as an embedded analytics provider, this process can be unreasonably slow and cumbersome. One solution is for users to export their data for further analysis elsewhere, but there are several disadvantages to this:

- Once the data is exported, the host application has lost any ability to manage, assure, or govern its quality or use.

- Decisions made and actions taken with this exported data can no longer be logged, audited, or analyzed along with the operational application.

- If users are regularly exporting data, especially for use in a business intelligence application, they are more likely to adopt that solution for analytics rather than your embedded options.

For these reasons and more, one colleague used to say, "Every time a user exports data, an angel loses its wings!"

It's helpful, therefore, if the embedded analytics platform can offer self-service capabilities that enable customers to create their own reports or dashboards without having to export data to a third-party application.

What do customers expect from self-service features in an embedded analytics platform?

Users should be able to reuse metrics and objects from the embedded environment and customize them simply. Advanced users need the capability to create completely new dashboards from scratch over the same dataset (and with the same connections and security) that the embedded application uses. This authoring experience should be supported with tools that enable simple but effective report and dashboard building.

 Self-service should be regarded as an advanced feature for a maturing embedded analytics product. In the first few releases, you should work closely with customers and users to understand what features they need, and then build those into the out-of-the-box product, rather than enabling extensive customization.

Although some embedded analytics platforms make it easy to enable customizations, that is not the end of the story. If a self-service user creates a custom object, report, or dashboard, you are now committed to support that customization through the lifetime of the product, with its numerous upgrades and new versions. Look for platforms that make the maintenance of customizations—not just the creation—simple, automated, and resilient.

Tiering an Analytics Product

We wrote earlier of the three integration patterns for embedded analytics: enhancements, new features, and new products. Each pattern has its own challenges and opportunities:

Enhanced features

It is difficult to charge customers extra for enhancements. They expect your product to continuously improve, and they expect more functionality in each release. Unless the analytic features mark a significant step-change in the use or value of your product, simple enhancements will generally be positioned as new competitive advantages rather than as new sources of revenue.

Analytics modules

On the other hand, more advanced features such as machine learning, self-service, and automation may be significant, but of value only to a subset of your market. In this case you may prefer to package these features separately as an analytic add-in or module, or provide an enhanced version with these features unlocked, for which you can charge an additional premium fee.

New analytics products

New products represent new lines of business. So, in addition to the technical work of ensuring integration and compatibility with your existing products, you also have some new business processes to deal with. A new product requires work from every department.

With these challenges in mind, how could you go about working out an appropriate price for embedded analytics?

A *tiered pricing model* is a pricing strategy that offers customers different levels of pricing for the same product or service, based on certain criteria such as volume or usage. This model helps incentivize customers to purchase more of a product or service, as the more they buy, the better the price. Tiered pricing can also be used to target different customer segments, allowing businesses to offer more competitive prices to more valuable customers.

Common tiers may be basic, professional, and enterprise, although there are many other labels. It's rare to find more than three tiers because users find it tricky to compare features and benefits across too many tiers. Three seems to be the sweet spot, and you may even have this structure in place for your existing SaaS offering.

How might you decide what goes into each tier?

The top tier of a tiered pricing model should generally include the most comprehensive and expensive products and services. For standalone products, this tier often includes features and benefits such as priority service and personalized attention;

customers might get dedicated account managers, priority response times, and access to specialized resources.

For an embedded product, the top tier could be factored in two ways. You could offer security and administration features that are most appropriate to global enterprises, or focus on scalability features. Alternatively, for any size of customer, you could offer advanced analytic features, such as machine learning or AI, as the top tier.

The Psychology of Tiered Products

Back in the 1960s, a family friend of one of the authors owned a pet shop. A popular product was bird seed, sold in bulk. There were three sacks displayed in the shop: budget, regular, and deluxe. Very few customers wanted to be mean to their pet birds, so the budget seed was only bought by people on a very tight budget. Equally, only the most indulgent bought the deluxe seed. A clear majority of people bought standard seed, but what they didn't know was that, except for the price, it was the same as budget seed with only a few token handfuls of extra sunflower seeds added per pound.

You should be a little more open with your customers, but on reflection you can see that their mindset will be similar. The entry-level tier is "basic" and, as a result, it may not be the tier they wish to run their business on, although it is good for experimenting and exploring the technology.

Conversely, the highest tier, "enterprise," may feel like overkill unless they really need those additional features.

As a result, your middle, or "professional," tier will be the most widely adopted. Think of this as the tier by which your product will be judged by customers, analysts, peers, and the market.

With a tiered model it's important to track carefully what tier people sign up for and how that changes over time. If too few people sign up for your top tier, it is most likely overpriced. However, if many people sign up for the top tier while few select the entry-level tier, your premium features are probably underpriced. Also, look for people moving up or down tiers, shifting their subscriptions: these are important price and value signals that can help you refactor tiers, make special offers, or choose how to position new features.

Tracking these behaviors is critical because your best returns will come from long-term relationships with your customers. You do not need to sell the most advanced capabilities straight away: customers who are successful will grow into more advanced tiers naturally and with greater confidence. They can start with a basic tier and progress through the analytics maturity model, with higher returns.

Alternatively, you may decide not to adopt a tiered model, but rather to offer a single set of features for all users. A good case for this approach is if you offer only enhanced features and want to use these enhancements for competitive differentiation from similarly priced products in the market. In this scenario, you would, in effect, absorb the cost of analytic features yourself. If that is unworkable, you could still charge for the analytic enhancements, but only offer one price point for all. But what should the price point be?

Pricing Embedded Analytics

If you are embedding analytic features into an existing software product, then you will have an existing pricing model. You may want to base your embedded analytics pricing on this model, but it can also make sense to try different approaches. Common examples are *competitive pricing*, where you position your product relative to the price of other products on the market, and *customer value pricing*, where you try to estimate how much your software is really worth to a customer in terms of the value they can get from it.

Competitive pricing is just what it sounds like: a pricing strategy in which a business sets its prices based on what its competitors are charging for the same or similar products or services. This strategy is commonly used in highly competitive markets, where a small difference in price can lead to significant changes in market share. Competitive pricing is usually focused on the short term, and businesses that use it must carefully monitor their competitors' prices and adjust their own accordingly.

For customer value pricing, consider the positive economic impact that your embedded analytics will have on customers. For example, determine if your new features offer them the ability to carry out tasks more efficiently, faster, or at a lower cost. This increases profit and reduces expenses. Improving customer satisfaction could be another measure, but it's more difficult to evaluate financially. Look for examples from real customers, such as case studies, to back up your claims.

If you have a limited number of customers who bring in a relatively large proportion of your revenue, then customer value pricing could be a beneficial solution. But as you can see, it can be hard to determine the right price, and this model can slow down your sales process because the value, and therefore the best price, may vary considerably from customer to customer.

If there are others in the market offering embedded analytics to your customers, then competitive pricing naturally makes sense. If you are first to the market with such features, then consider customer value pricing. But still, you must monitor your own and your competitors' performance closely and be willing to adjust as needed.

Supporting Embedded Analytics

The key question to answer when looking at how you will support your embedded solution is this: who will provide first tier and second tier customer support?

First tier customer support is the initial point of contact and can include phone, email, and chat support. First tier customer service agents are responsible for responding to customer inquiries, troubleshooting technical issues, and providing basic information.

Second tier customer support is the next level of customer service and typically involves dealing with more technical issues and more detailed troubleshooting. This support is often provided by more experienced customer service agents or may involve more specialized teams.

Customer support agents typically pass issues from first tier support to second tier support by escalating the issue in a ticket system and then assigning it to a support agent with a higher level of expertise. Some customer support systems also allow agents to assign ticket priority levels, which can help ensure that complex or urgent issues are handled quickly.

If you are using a third-party platform for embedded analytics, rather than building your own, you will need to be clear what the support processes are. How will you escalate issues to the third-party vendor, and what are its service level agreements (SLAs)?

Tackle these process questions early. You don't want to work this out in production!

Launching Your Product

As you will know from your existing products, there are many things you should prepare for a new launch. For embedded analytics specifically, you will need to consider the following:

Service level agreements
> If your contracts don't align with the guarantees of your analytics platform provider, you should be sure to understand their SLAs, disaster recovery protocols, and so on. You may need to adjust your contracts and work with your legal team to determine the correct approach.

Data privacy and regulatory compliance
> As described in Chapter 7, you will need advice from your legal team to understand the applicable data privacy regulations. The team will likely have to research applicable laws and regulations to determine what is required for your product to be compliant. You can then develop a data protection policy that outlines how you will collect, use, store, and protect customer data. Be

transparent about this. Provide customers with clear information about how their data will be used and protected.

Billing and subscriptions

You will likely need to make modifications to your billing and subscription procedures to properly charge clients for the new product, regardless of the tiering and pricing model you choose. Be sure to consider that over the long term you want customers in a tiered product offering to move up the value chain to the premium level. How will they do that? With most vendors, the finance team will advise you on billing and subscriptions. You will need their help.

Marketing readiness

It's good to work with marketing early in the product cycle so they can be well prepared for launch. The marketing team will be responsible for obvious tasks, such as preparing social media and updating your website and collateral, but will also need to work with press and industry analysts to raise awareness of the new capabilities. Especially when dealing with analysts, this can be a lengthy process that often starts with the early beta releases.

Sales readiness

This includes training sales reps on the product features, benefits, and key selling points, as well as providing them with the necessary sales materials and tools to successfully demonstrate the product and close deals. It also involves creating strategies to target the right customer base and defining processes to track and measure success.

Training materials

In addition to the documentation already mentioned, most products need a range of user-friendly training materials. For consistency, these should align in style and presentation with your existing materials. Demo videos showing the product's features, functions, and benefits are always popular. For some tasks you may need step-by-step tutorials. There is a fuzzy area between some marketing material and training material, especially when it comes to rich media content like videos. Webinars, live or recorded, can provide an in-depth overview of the product for training, but also serve to raise awareness and provide excellent lead generation.

With these actions prepared, you can choose to launch your embedded analytics features in one of two ways: aligned with a version update of your existing product, or as a separate launch. Which of these makes sense will depend on whether you are shipping embedded analytics as new features, new modules, or as a new product.

Whatever course of action you choose, we are sure this launch will be an exciting and impactful moment for your organization.

Conclusion

From simple reporting to the most advanced algorithmic insights, analytics adds a great deal of value to almost any software product. The ability to make informed and timely decisions to optimize operations and performance can be transformative in itself. Embedded analytics enables businesses to gain insights into customer behavior, market trends, and areas of opportunity at the point of decision.

This highly proactive approach integrated into existing products adds so much value that we believe in many cases it is worth considering as a business opportunity in its own right. Implemented as new features, embedded analytics affords an opportunity to revisit existing pricing models and product tiers to maximize the long-term value for customers. As new modules, or even as new products or SKUs, this opportunity is even greater.

With embedded analytics in place, you are not just a data business; you are offering insight and intelligence within your products. You will be an analytics business, and, we trust, with the help of this book, a highly successful one.

Index

A

adaptable options, security, 75
administration, 69-81
    console user interface, 80
    deployment, 69-71
    DevOps, 71-74, 79
    report bursting, 79
    scheduling, 79
    security, 75-78
    tools, 27
    version management, 79
aggregated measures, KPIs as, 48
aggregation tables, 40
AI (see artificial intelligence, probability and data ambiguity)
Airtable, 107
ambiguity and analytics, 19-20
analytic objects, embedding
    data visualizations, 49-52
    dynamic text and NLG content, 54
    iframes, 58-60
    interactivity, 55-58
    key performance indicators, 48
    tabular data, 53
analytics engine, 23
analytics maturity model, 114, 135
analytics modules, analytics product, 134
APIs for embedded analytics integrations, 33, 40, 78
architectures, 23-36
    administration tools, 27
    analytics engine, 23
    branding and user experience, 24
    business intelligence applications, 32-33

component libraries, 28-29
data connectivity, 23
developer resources, 25
enterprise reporting, 30-32
purpose-built embedded, 34-35
scalability, 26
security, 27
self-service analytics, 35
artificial intelligence (AI), probability and data ambiguity, 19
    (see also data science and machine learning)
asset, treating data as, 127-129
awareness, governance program, 88

B

banding of reports for clarity, 31
Bates, Marcia, 13
BI (see business intelligence)
billing and subscriptions, product launch, 138
branding and user experience, 24
bulk connector, 40
business considerations, 127-139
    asset, data as, 127-129
    data products, 129-138
    embedded analytics integrations, 65
    executive and strategic decisions, 10
    launching the product, 137-138
    measurable outcomes of embedded analytics for, 4
    pricing the product, 136
    product analytics systems, 131-132
    security and privacy of continuity, 91
    self-service as feature, 132-133
    support function, 137

tiered model of product, 134-136
business intelligence (BI)
    applications/software, 32-33
    embedded analytics approach, 1
    in-memory application popularity, 42
    limits of, 4, 12
    self-service analytics, 35
    spreadsheet tool as data source, 5

C

caching model, impact on response times, 57
call center use case, DSML, 117-123
    end user experience test, 121-123
    propensity modeling, 118
    putting model into practice, 120
    training a model, 118-120
chart-based visualizations, 49-52
CI/CD (continuous integration/continuous
    delivery) process, 73
closed system, 76
cloud deployment, 70-71, 73, 91
cloud governance, 90
Coetzee, J. M., 19
Colaboratory, 108
collaboration's benefits for governance, 88
competitive pricing, 136
compliance team, 87
compliance, regulatory, 85-87, 137
component libraries, 28-29
computation support for large data volumes,
    104
computational notebooks, 108-109
concurrency impact on embedded content, 57
connectivity, operational databases and, 39
console user interface, administrative, 80
consumers, embedded analytics for, 3, 65
container software, 73, 74
content curation, DSML, 124
content management, programmatic, 67
continuous integration/continuous delivery
    (CI/CD) process, 73
CORS (cross-origin resource sharing), 60
CRM (customer relationship management)
    platforms, 53, 56
cross-domain/origin limitations of iframes, 59
cross-functional team for security and privacy,
    90
cross-origin resource sharing (CORS), 60
CSV and other text file formats, 37-38

customer journey optimization, DSML, 124
customer relationship management (CRM)
    platforms, 53, 56
customer support for analytics product, 137
customer value pricing, 136
customizations, upgrading for self-service ana-
    lytics, 35

D

D3.js, 28
data, 37-45
    analytic data sources, 41-43
    as asset, 127-129
    connectivity element, 23
    data integration pipelines, 43
    decision support role of, 10-13
    delimited, 37-38, 96
    downloading for targeted use cases, 110
    operational data sources, 39-40
    raw, 96
    sharing, 60, 104
    tabular, 53, 96
    value of self-service to avoid export costs,
        133
    volume issue for Excel, 104
    writing back to sources, 18, 43, 64-65
data definition language (DDL), 114
data governance (see governance)
data hoarding, avoiding, 88
data integration pipelines, 43
data lakehouses, 42
data lakes, 42
data marts, 41
data products, 129-138
    launching the product, 137-138
    pricing of embedded analytics, 136
    self-service as a feature, 132-133
    support function, 137
    tiered model of product, 134-136
data scenarios, DevOps/analytics best practices,
    73
data science and machine learning (DSML),
    113-126
    in analytics practice, 113-117
    call center use case, 117-123
    generative language services, 125-126
    predictive analytics, 115, 118-123
    prescriptive analytics, 63, 115, 123
    use case examples, 121-125

in-memory analytics engines, 26, 32, 42, 43
interactivity with data
    adding to analytic objects, 17, 55-58
    BI applications and, 32
    consistent methods for, 110
IT operations, 71-74
    advantages of embedded analytics, 2
    building embedded analytics to serve, 28
    from gatekeepers to shopkeepers, 86
    self-service analytics and, 35, 86, 132-133
    version management, 79

K

kernel, in collaborative notebook, 109
key performance indicators (KPIs), 48
Kubernetes, 74

L

launching the product, 137-138
line charts, 49
lineage and impact analysis, 66
load balancing, 71
logging features, to enhance security, 27, 78

M

machine learning operations (MLOps), 114
marketing readiness, product launch, 138
measurable business outcomes, 4, 92
metadata, CSV file access limitation, 38
Microsoft Power BI, 42, 113
middle management decision making, 12
MLOps (machine learning operations), 114
monday.com, 107
multitenant support, security consideration, 75

N

natural language processing/generation (NLP/
    NLG) tools, 54, 125-126
navigation, user interactivity with data, 55
navigational scope of embedded analytics, 16
network graph theory, 117
new analytics products, in tiered product, 134
NLP/NLG (natural language processing/gener-
    ation) tools, 54, 125-126

O

OLAP (online analytic processing), 24, 64
OLTP (online transaction processing), 64

on-premises deployment, 69
online analytic processing (OLAP), 24, 64
online transaction processing (OLTP), 64
open system, 76
openness, governance program, 88
operational applications/workflow integration,
    18, 34
operational data sources, 39-40
operational decisions, 11-13
operationalization (write-back) of data, 18, 43,
    64-65
orientation step, decision making, 13
outliers, 14

P

parsing of data, CSV limitations with BI tools,
    38
pattern recognition, human talent for, 99
performance
    interactive analytics considerations, 57
    optimizations for text files, 38
permissions, security considerations, 27, 75
personnel dimension, data warehouse, 41
pie charts, 51
platforms, 28-35
    business intelligence applications, 32-33
    component libraries, 28-29
    CRM, 53, 56
    enterprise reporting, 30-32
    ERP, 49, 53, 65
    purpose-built embedded, 34-35
    self-service analytics, 35, 42, 86, 132-133
    spreadsheets as, 5, 100-105
point-in-time restores for cloud backups, 91
Power BI, 42, 113
predictive analytics, 115, 118-123
prescriptive analytics, 63, 115, 123
pricing of embedded analytics, 136
privacy
    governance and, 85, 90-91
    product launch consideration, 137
    taking responsibility for customer, 87
product analytics systems, 131-132
product experience, interactivity as value-add
    for, 56
products, data (see data products)
programmatic content management, 67
programmatic control of user provisioning, 67

third-party standards integration, security, 76
tiered pricing model of analytics product, 134-136
time dimension, data warehouse, 41
training a model, call center use case, 118-120
training materials, product launch, 138
training, governance program, 88

U

uncertainty and analytics, 19-20
user optimization for purchase, DSML, 124
user provisioning, programmatic control of, 67

V

value pricing, 136
version management, 79
vertical scaling, 73
view tables, 40
virtual machines (VMs), 74
visual analytics, 95-111
    computational notebooks, 108-109
    integration and collaboration, 107

planning the move to, 95-96
as primary solution, 109
project management and workflow, 107
simple reporting and analytics, 105-107
spreadsheets and (see spreadsheets)
visual enumeration, human talent for, 97-98
visualizations, data
    best practice, 61
    component libraries, 28-29
    decision-making role, 15-16
    embedding analytic objects, 49-52
    operational workflow integration, 18
    trends in, 61
    value for data products, 129
VMs (virtual machines), 74

W

web analytics, 131
web applications, embedding capability, 27
white labeling of user experience, 24
workflow embedding, 18, 34, 61-65, 107
write-back of data, 18, 43, 64-65

About the Authors

Donald Farmer is the principal of TreeHive Strategy, a strategic advisory practice specializing in data, analytics, and innovation strategy. His background is very diverse, with over 30 years of deeply practical experience in industries ranging from fish farming to archaeology to advanced manufacturing. He has worked in award-winning startups in the UK and Iceland, and spent 15 years at Microsoft and Qlik leading teams designing and developing new enterprise capabilities in data integration, data mining, self-service analytics, and visualization.

Donald is an advisor to investors, venture funds, incubators, and startups around the world. He mentors executives and speaks globally at events and private workshops. He lives with his wife, Alison, an artist, in a recycled-polystyrene house near Seattle with one of the world's most beautiful tree houses—the tree hive—in their wild garden.

Jim Horbury is solutions practice director at InterWorks, currently living and working in Hampshire, UK. Having spent almost two decades working in technical and creative direction roles in advertising, Jim was an early proponent of data-driven response measurement and drove the development of ad-tech reporting solutions for some of the UK's largest travel and tourism organizations.

After a move into telecoms, big data, and machine learning, it was a natural step to put his accumulated knowledge into action as a consultant. Jim now leads a global team of solution architects working with some of the world's best-known brands, designing and leading the development of innovative and scalable analytics solutions.

Outside of work, Jim tries to recapture his youth with mountain biking, running, and climbing.

Colophon

The animal on the cover of *Embedded Analytics* is a horned parakeet (*Eunymphicus cornutus*).

This festively arrayed, medium-size parrot is native to the islands of New Caledonia in the South Pacific, where it is found primarily in remnant tracts of rainforest but may also inhabit savanna or shrubland.

These birds are often observed in the forest canopy, foraging for nuts and seeds in pairs or small groups, or occupying nests on or near the ground or in tree hollows. Interestingly, they are distinguished among most parrots for a rare nest-sharing behavior, in which two individuals may simultaneously incubate their eggs in the same nest.

As shown in the cover illustration, horned parakeets display a vibrant plumage of green with some yellow, red, blue, and black, and their heads are surmounted by two black, red-tipped feathers, or "horns." Adult individuals average around 12–14 inches in length from head to tail and command a wide range of vocalizations, from raucous (*https://oreil.ly/1a9Ts*) to subdued.

Unfortunately, horned parakeets have been categorized by the IUCN as vulnerable, due to a small total population (around five thousand individuals) with declines since the 1880s resulting from habitat degradation. Many of the animals on O'Reilly covers are endangered; all of them are important to the world.

The cover illustration is by Karen Montgomery, based on an antique line engraving from *Histoire Naturelle*. The cover fonts are Gilroy Semibold and Guardian Sans. The text font is Adobe Minion Pro; the heading font is Adobe Myriad Condensed; and the code font is Dalton Maag's Ubuntu Mono.